Artificial Intelligence & Generative AI for Beginners:

The Complete Guide

BUNDLE: 3 Books in 1

David M. Patel

Table of Contents

FOREWORD

Let me simply ask you...

- So, you've heard of Generative AI and find yourself wondering what all the fuss is about?

- Have you stumbled upon ChatGPT and questioned the extent of its capabilities?

- As a creator, are you curious about how Generative AI could revolutionize your industry?

- Do you find yourself itching to play with the most cutting-edge Generative AI tools but don't know where to start?

- Are you curious about how AI tools like Adobe Firefly or Google Bard are being used to shape creative processes and industries?

- Or perhaps, you're pondering the ethical implications of Generative AI and want to understand the full picture?

If you found yourself nodding along to any of these questions, you're in the right place. This book, "Artificial Intelligence and Generative AI for Beginners," is crafted precisely for you!

Just a few months ago, I found myself in a similar situation. I had started to explore generative AI tools like ChatGPT, Adobe Firefly, and Google Bard, and found myself awed by their capabilities and the enormous potential they held. And yet, I was acutely aware that many users were missing out, confused or even intimidated by these powerful tools.

This book is my earnest attempt to bridge that gap.

The exciting world of AI and Generative AI is no longer just a playground for tech enthusiasts or scientists—it is accessible to all of us. And this accessibility brings with it the potential for sweeping change, led not by a select few, but by everyone who dares to embrace this technology.

Our journey in these pages will cover the basics of AI, its wide-ranging applications, and dive deep into the fascinating world of Generative AI. The tech-talk has been kept simple, the anecdotes relatable. This isn't just a book about learning AI—it is about understanding its role in our lives and future, especially the transformative power of Generative AI.

We won't merely discuss how Generative AI can transform industries—we will delve into real, tangible examples. Whether you're a budding entrepreneur, a seasoned professional, or an impassioned creator, you'll find valuable insights that directly apply to your field.

As we navigate this exciting territory, we won't shy away from the difficult conversations. As much as Generative AI holds promise, it also brings forth complex ethical questions about bias, privacy, and job displacement. These are conversations we need to have, and this book will serve as your guide.

Your journey into the world of generative AI starts here. It is time to turn the page, step into the future, and unlock the mysteries of generative AI together. Welcome aboard!

Sincerely,
David M. Patel

INTRODUCTION

Welcome to the thrilling journey through the realms of artificial intelligence (AI) and its creatively inspiring subset, generative AI. This introductory segment is designed to usher you into the dynamic world of AI, showcasing its evolution, varied forms, and profound societal impacts.

In its simplest form, AI is a multifaceted discipline aiming to build intelligent machines capable of mimicking human cognitive functions—thinking, learning, problem-solving, perception, and language understanding. Essentially, AI seeks to forge intelligent entities that perform tasks otherwise reliant on human intellect.

The narrative of AI has dramatically shifted over the years, transitioning from an obscure, niche field to a mainstream phenomenon, causing seismic changes across countless industries. Today, AI pervades our lives—from virtual assistants like Siri and Alexa, to recommendation algorithms powering Netflix and Amazon, and even autonomous driving technology. The launch of ChatGPT in November 2022 marked a transformative moment in AI history, introducing the compelling concept of Generative AI to the world. Since then, the discourse around Generative AI has expanded explosively, as more people grapple with its potentials and seek ways to benefit from a growing suite of remarkable generative AI solutions unveiled daily.

AI has transcended its role as a simple tool, reshaping the way we work, live, and problem-solve. Its extraordinary learning capabilities, adaptability to new inputs, and performance of human-like tasks have made it indispensable in diverse sectors. Today, this transformative technology is impacting healthcare, education, transportation, entertainment, and beyond.

The central aim of this book is to offer a comprehensive beginner's guide to AI, with a spotlight on Generative AI—a revolutionary approach that empowers computers to design, iterate, and evaluate generated content, like images, sound,

3

and text, far more rapidly than any human could.

As we traverse this book, we will unveil the many facets of AI and Generative AI, demystify how they operate, their real-world applications, and their potential future trajectory. Regardless of whether you are an AI enthusiast, student, business leader, or merely intrigued by the field, this book is designed to equip you with a robust understanding of AI and Generative AI.

In the following chapters, we'll start with the foundational concepts of AI, gradually immersing ourselves in the intricate world of Generative AI, peppered with practical examples and real-world applications. By the end of this intellectual expedition, you will not only have a comprehensive understanding of AI and Generative AI but also the ability to critically evaluate their implications for our collective future.

Ready? Let's take a deep dive into the captivating ocean of AI, starting with its basic principles.…...

PART I: ARTIFICIAL INTELLIGENCE FOR BEGINNERS

CHAPTER 1: UNDERSTANDING AI

Understanding the absolute basics of AI is an essential and important step to lay the groundwork for the later chapters of this book. If you already have a solid understanding of AI, this chapter is going to serve as a useful reminder. If you are absolutely new to the world of AI, then this chapter is a great starting point. This chapter is designed to provide a broad overview of AI, its history, and the different types that have been developed over the years. We will delve into the past, tracing back the roots of AI, and gradually move forward to the present to understand the various types of AI that exist today.

Whether you're an aspiring tech enthusiast, a professional looking to switch careers, or simply someone intrigued by AI, this chapter will lay a solid foundation for your AI knowledge.

1.1 AI Basics

Artificial Intelligence, commonly abbreviated as AI, is a multifaceted discipline within the larger field of computer science. Its overarching goal is to devise systems that can perform tasks requiring human intelligence — such systems are built to perceive their environment, interpret data, learn from experiences, and make decisions much like a human would.

The notion of AI is anchored on the concept of building 'intelligent agents.' An intelligent agent, in the context of AI, is any system that perceives its environment through sensors and interacts with it through actuators, guided by specific objectives. It is an entity that senses, understands, learns, plans, and can actuate to meet its goals.

Consider a self-driving car, one of the more complex examples of AI. Such a vehicle perceives its surroundings via a host of sensors, including LIDAR, radar, and cameras. It then processes this data, identifies patterns, and makes decisions about the direction to take, speed to maintain, when to stop, and more. It continues to learn from these interactions, adjusting its future behavior based on past experiences — all hallmarks of an intelligent agent.

But AI isn't just about high-stakes applications like autonomous driving. It is also nestled quietly in our everyday lives, enhancing our experiences and making tasks easier. The AI in your smartphone's personal assistant, for instance, processes your voice commands, learns your habits, and assists with tasks, ranging from setting alarms and sending texts to providing real-time traffic updates and suggesting new music.

Online, AI powers the recommendation engines of e-commerce and entertainment platforms. It takes note of your browsing and purchasing habits, learning your preferences over time. Based on this learning, it recommends products you might like or movies you might enjoy.

In essence, AI is the force behind a rapidly increasing range of applications, driving innovation, and improving efficiency across industries and aspects of our everyday lives. This technology, with its ability to mimic human intelligence, brings the promise of revolutionizing every field it touches, from healthcare and education to finance, transportation, and entertainment.

AI has the potential to facilitate personalized learning in education by adapting to each student's pace and style of learning. In healthcare, it could democratize access to quality care and improve outcomes with personalized treatment plans based on a patient's unique genetics and lifestyle. In transportation, AI could usher in an era of safer, more efficient mobility with self-driving cars. In finance, AI can provide more secure, seamless transactions, and more accurate risk assessment for loans and insurance.

However, despite its immense potential, AI is a field still in its infancy and comes with significant challenges. One of the critical challenges of AI is the 'black box' problem — the lack of transparency in how AI systems make decisions. As AI systems become more complex, their decision-making processes become less transparent, leading to issues related to trust and accountability.

Then there's the issue of data privacy. AI systems, especially those based on machine learning, require vast amounts of data for training. This raises concerns about the privacy and security of individuals' data. Legislation like the General Data Protection Regulation (GDPR) in the EU is already addressing this issue, but it remains a significant concern.

Bias is another issue. AI systems learn from the data they are fed. If this data is biased, the systems can reinforce and perpetuate these biases, leading to unfair outcomes.

Moreover, there are ethical questions surrounding AI's impact on jobs and society at large. While AI is expected to create new jobs, it is also likely to render certain jobs obsolete, raising questions about the future of work in an AI-driven world.

1.2 The History of AI

From humble beginnings in the early 1950s, Artificial Intelligence (AI) has grown into a pervasive technology, one that shapes our everyday lives and promises to revolutionize the world. Its development, mirroring the evolution of computing itself, is a compelling story of ingenuity, vision, hard work, and a bit of fortune.

A. The Birth of AI: 1950s to 1970s

In 1950, British mathematician and computer scientist Alan Turing published a groundbreaking paper entitled "Computing Machinery and Intelligence," which proposed what is now known as the Turing Test. This test assesses a machine's ability to exhibit intelligent behavior equivalent to or indistinguishable from a human's. The paper started a new conversation about the possibilities of machine intelligence.

In 1956, the Dartmouth Conference marked the birth of AI as a field. John McCarthy, Marvin Minsky, Allen Newell, and Herbert Simon, the founding fathers of AI, defined AI as "the science and engineering of making intelligent machines." From there, the dream of creating an artificial brain took off.

One significant event in the early days of AI was the development of the General Problem Solver (GPS) in 1957 by Allen Newell and Herbert Simon. The GPS was a computer program designed to mimic human problem-solving strategies. This early AI system was followed by the invention of the perceptron, an algorithm for supervised learning of binary classifiers, by Frank Rosenblatt in 1958.

The 1960s and 70s were full of exploratory research and development in AI, focusing on knowledge-based systems and the first autonomous robots. These included Shakey the Robot, developed by SRI International in 1966, one of the first robots that could analyze and react to its surroundings.

During the 1970s, the limitations of the then AI became apparent, leading to a period known as the "AI Winter." Funding was reduced, and interest waned due to the lack of practical, scalable applications. However, these early trials and tribulations laid the groundwork for the advancements that were to come.

B. AI Comes of Age: 1980s to 2000s

AI research was reignited in the 1980s with the advent of expert systems, which used knowledge from domain experts to mimic human decision-making. XCON, developed by Carnegie Mellon University, was a notable early expert system that saved millions of dollars by assisting in the configuration of computer systems.

Meanwhile, the 1980s also saw the rise of machine learning. In 1986, Rumelhart, Hinton, and Williams introduced backpropagation for training multi-layer neural networks, breathing new life into neural network research.

In the late 90s and early 2000s, AI began to infiltrate our everyday lives. In 1997, IBM's Deep Blue, a chess-playing computer, defeated the reigning world chess champion, Garry Kasparov. This was a significant milestone, demonstrating that AI could outperform humans at complex tasks.

Meanwhile, advancements in data storage and processing capabilities paved the way for data-driven AI techniques. The development of support vector machines, decision trees, and ensemble methods marked significant progress in the field of machine learning.

Deep Learning Revolution

In the early 2010s, the re-emergence of neural networks—specifically, deep neural networks—led to a new age of AI, marked by significant advancements in machine learning capabilities.

A pivotal moment came in 2012, when AlexNet, a deep neural network designed by Krizhevsky, Sutskever, and Hinton, won the ImageNet Large Scale Visual Recognition Challenge, a competition for object recognition algorithms. It significantly outperformed the second-best competitor and shook the AI world. The victory marked the start of the "deep learning revolution," a shift towards using deep neural networks to solve complex AI tasks.

Breakthroughs in Game Playing

Artificial intelligence achieved significant milestones in game-playing during this period, demonstrating its growing capabilities. In 2015, AlphaGo, a program developed by Google's DeepMind, defeated a professional human player at the game of Go, a feat thought to be years away due to the game's complexity. AlphaGo used a combination of machine learning and tree search techniques, along with extensive training from both human and computer-played games.

In 2017, an improved version called AlphaGo Zero learned to play simply by playing against itself, without any prior knowledge except the game's rules. By doing so, it achieved superhuman performance, even defeating its predecessor 100 games to 0.

Evolution of Language Models

During this period, significant strides were also made in natural language processing (NLP), especially with the development of transformer-based models. The attention mechanism, introduced by Vaswani et al. in 2017 in the "Attention is All You Need" paper, became a fundamental component of many NLP models, enabling better understanding of language context and sequence.

This period also saw the advent of OpenAI's GPT models. Starting with GPT-1 in 2018, these models utilized transformers to generate coherent and contextually relevant sentences. GPT-3, launched in 2020, was a landmark in AI for its impressive performance in generating human-like text. In 2022, OpenAI released ChatGPT, a conversational AI based on the GPT-3 model, that could conduct detailed conversations with users in a coherent and contextually aware manner.

Generative AI Developments

Generative AI has seen remarkable progress in recent years, thanks to advances in deep learning and hardware. Some notable examples include:

In 2017, Nvidia developed Progressive Growing of GANs (ProGAN), a technique that gradually increased the size of the network and training data to improve the quality and resolution of generated images. The following year, Nvidia introduced StyleGAN, a variant of GANs that enabled the generation of highly realistic human faces with precise control over attributes and styles.

In 2019, OpenAI unveiled MuseNet, a deep neural network capable of generating original music across various genres and styles. Probably the most important milestone in 2020 was when OpenAI released DALL-E, an impressive generative AI system that used GPT-3 as its foundation to create images based on text descriptions, combining the talents of Salvador Dali and WALL-E in its name.

More recently, in 2021, Stability AI made its AI-powered design studio Stable Diffusion (SD) open source, utilizing diffusion models to generate images based on text descriptions, opening up new possibilities for creative expression.

Autonomous AI Systems

Meanwhile, autonomous AI systems also began to flourish. AI's growing proficiency at perception and decision-making tasks facilitated the development of self-driving cars. Tesla, Waymo, and Cruise, among others, began extensive testing of autonomous vehicles on public roads. AI's applications also expanded into other areas, such as drones and robotics, leading to innovations like Boston Dynamics' humanoid robots and Amazon's delivery drones.

AI in Healthcare

AI's applications in healthcare also saw significant progress. Machine learning models were developed for tasks like diagnosing diseases, predicting the outcomes patients would face, and personalizing treatment plans. For instance:

In 2018, Google's DeepMind developed an AI system that could diagnose eye diseases as accurately as expert human doctors. The most important milestone in 2019 was IBM's Watson Health launching Watson for Genomics Precision Oncology (WGPO), an AI system that could analyze genomic data and recommend personalized cancer treatments based on clinical evidence.

In 2020, Google's DeepMind developed AlphaFold 2 (AF2), a deep learning system that could predict the three-dimensional structure of proteins with unprecedented accuracy and speed, solving one of the grand challenges of biology and opening new possibilities for drug discovery and biotechnology.

As we stand in 2023, the progress made in AI from the 2010s to the present is remarkable. From deep learning to game-playing, from natural language understanding to generative AI, from autonomous systems to healthcare, AI has come a long way in a relatively short time. The leaps and bounds made in this period have set a promising precedent for the future of AI.

1.3 Different Types of AI

Artificial Intelligence can be broadly categorized into three types based on its capabilities: Narrow AI, General AI, and Superintelligent AI. Each of these categories represents different stages of AI's potential development and capabilities.

1.3.1 Narrow AI

Narrow AI, also known as Weak AI, represents AI systems that are designed to perform a specific task, and their functionality doesn't extend beyond that specific task. While the term "weak" might suggest inferiority, it is important to note that it only refers to the specialization of these systems, not their capabilities. In fact, Narrow AI systems can outperform humans in their specific tasks. This chapter delves into the mechanics, applications, and implications of Narrow AI.

1.3.1.1 The Essence of Narrow AI

Narrow AI operates within a limited context. Unlike general AI, it doesn't possess understanding or consciousness; rather, it is designed to perform a predetermined task with a high degree of specialization. It doesn't possess the ability to apply knowledge from one domain to another.

Narrow AI leverages a variety of AI techniques, including machine learning, deep learning, and natural language processing, depending on its designated task. It is the type of AI that we encounter most frequently in our everyday lives, often without realizing it.

1.3.1.2 Narrow AI in our Daily Lives: An In-Depth Look

Narrow AI is increasingly embedded in the fabric of our daily lives, providing us with smart solutions in numerous sectors. Here are more detailed insights into some prominent examples:

Personal Assistants

Personal virtual assistants like Siri, Alexa, and Google Assistant are perhaps some of the most familiar examples of Narrow AI. They use natural language processing and voice recognition technologies to understand and respond to user commands.

Despite their ability to carry out an impressive array of tasks, such as setting reminders, answering questions, and controlling other smart devices, their functionalities are strictly limited to what they've been programmed for. They do not understand the context beyond their programming and cannot make decisions independently.

Recommendation Systems

Recommendation systems, like those utilized by Amazon or Netflix, are another prevalent example of Narrow AI. These systems employ machine learning algorithms to analyze user behavior and preferences, predict potential interests, and recommend relevant items or content.

While these recommendation systems may seem to understand user preferences remarkably well, they are simply pattern recognition systems. They don't understand the items they recommend, nor do they comprehend user preferences beyond the correlations in the data they've been trained on.

Autonomous Vehicles

Autonomous vehicles represent a complex and advanced application of Narrow AI. Companies like Tesla and Waymo have developed self-driving cars that use a combination of computer vision, sensor technology, and machine learning to navigate roads, interpret traffic signs, and avoid obstacles.

However, despite their advanced capabilities, these AI systems are still considered Narrow AI. They are singularly focused on the task of driving and don't possess the ability to apply their learned knowledge to other contexts.

1.3.1.3 The Implications and Limitations of Narrow AI

As we increasingly rely on Narrow AI to automate and optimize various aspects of our lives, it is crucial to be aware of its implications and limitations.

Advancements and Impact

The rapid advancements in Narrow AI have undoubtedly created significant benefits. Automation of repetitive tasks, personalized recommendations, enhanced data analysis, and prediction capabilities are some of the positive impacts that have transformed businesses and improved user experiences.

Narrow AI has also made strides in healthcare, with AI models that can diagnose diseases with high accuracy. In environmental conservation, AI models help track wildlife populations and identify areas at high risk of deforestation.

However, despite these advancements, Narrow AI is not without its challenges and limitations.

Limitations

The foremost limitation of Narrow AI is its inability to perform beyond its specific programming. It cannot make decisions independently or understand context outside of its designated task. For instance, a chess-playing AI, however advanced, cannot use its chess strategies to play another game like poker or to comprehend human emotions. Another limitation lies in the quality and quantity of data needed to train Narrow AI systems. These systems require vast amounts of labeled data to learn effectively. The collection and labeling of such data can be time-consuming and expensive. Moreover, the reliance on data also raises privacy concerns, as personal data is often used in training these AI models.

1.3.2 General AI – AGI (Artificial General Intelligence)

General AI, otherwise known as Strong AI or Artificial General Intelligence (AGI), is a level of machine intelligence that can fully emulate a human being's intelligence. Unlike Narrow AI, AGI would possess the capability to understand, learn, apply knowledge, and improve itself autonomously across a broad range of tasks. This advanced form of AI would not be confined to a specific task but could intelligently navigate through multiple complex tasks just like a human.

1.3.2.1 Conceptual Framework and Functioning

In an ideal scenario, AGI would mimic human cognitive abilities. It would not just execute tasks or solve problems within a specific domain, but exhibit a wide-ranging understanding of various contexts, exhibit common sense reasoning, adapt to new situations, and learn from experience. This level of AI would engage in general problem-solving, make decisions under uncertainty, plan for the future, and learn new knowledge without needing explicit programming.

1.3.2.2 The Potential of General AI

The realization of General AI would potentially be a monumental breakthrough, bringing substantial changes to various sectors and society at large. AGI could take over complex problem-solving tasks, make accurate predictions, automate decision-making processes, and drive innovation across fields including but not limited to healthcare, climate modeling, research, and economic planning.

1.3.2.3 Challenges in Achieving General AI

Despite the potential, the development of AGI presents numerous challenges:

1.3.2.3.1 Technical Challenges

Creating an AI system with human-like cognition demands massive computational power and significant advancements in algorithms and architectures. Achieving a broad understanding and knowledge similar to human intelligence, encapsulating common sense reasoning, creativity, and emotional intelligence, requires fundamental breakthroughs in AI research.

1.3.2.3.2 Ethical and Safety Concerns

The development of AGI also raises profound ethical and safety issues. An autonomous, self-learning, and self-improving system might behave in unpredictable ways that could pose risks. Addressing these concerns involves finding solutions to align AGI's goals with human values, developing robust and safe systems, and ensuring the system's actions remain beneficial if it self-improves beyond its original capabilities.

1.3.2.3.3 Societal Impact

Concerns also extend to the societal impact of AGI. Job displacement due to automation, concentration of power, privacy, and security are issues that need careful handling. Ensuring that the benefits of AGI are distributed fairly across society is a significant challenge.

As of now, despite significant strides in AI, AGI remains largely theoretical and unattained. However, research continues in pursuit of this fascinating and complex goal. The journey towards AGI is fraught with challenges, but also filled with tremendous potential. It represents not just the frontier of technological innovation, but also a profound quest to understand and replicate the intricacies of human intelligence.

1.3.3 Superintelligent AI

Superintelligent AI, a concept popularized by philosopher Nick Bostrom, refers to an AI that surpasses human intelligence and ability in virtually every economically valuable work. This would not just include intellectual tasks like problem-solving and creativity, but also social skills like persuasion and negotiation.

1.3.3.1 The Promise and Perils of Superintelligence

Like General AI, Superintelligent AI is still within the realm of theory and science fiction. If realized, it could potentially solve humanity's most challenging problems, such as climate change and disease. However, it could also pose significant risks. The challenge of controlling an entity smarter than ourselves raises numerous safety and ethical concerns that researchers have yet to fully address.

The discussion around Superintelligent AI can often seem like pure speculation. After all, we're talking about a form of intelligence that not only matches but greatly surpasses human intelligence, and we're not there yet. However, it is a topic that's drawing increasing attention from scientists, philosophers, and tech leaders.

1.3.3.2. The Potential Benefits of Superintelligent AI

The potential benefits of Superintelligent AI are vast. If realized, such an AI could potentially help us solve some of the most complex and intractable problems facing humanity.

Climate Change: Superintelligent AI could significantly advance our understanding of complex systems like climate, helping us develop effective strategies to mitigate climate change. It could optimize renewable energy systems, develop advanced materials for carbon capture, and model the ecological impacts of different policy decisions with unprecedented accuracy.

Disease: In the medical field, Superintelligent AI could lead to breakthroughs in our understanding of diseases and the human body. It could sift through vast amounts of medical data to find patterns that humans would miss, leading to new treatments and possibly even cures.

Technological Progress: More broadly, Superintelligent AI could accelerate technological progress in general, leading to breakthroughs we can't yet imagine. It could optimize designs, manage complex logistical problems, and make scientific discoveries at a pace far beyond human capability.

1.3.3.3 The Risks of Superintelligent AI

While the potential benefits are tremendous, so too are the risks. These are concerns that we must start addressing now, well before such an AI becomes a reality.

Existential Risk: Philosophers like Nick Bostrom argue that Superintelligent AI could pose an existential risk to humanity. This is because such an AI could become so powerful that it would be impossible for humans to control. If its goals aren't aligned with ours, it could cause immense harm.

Ethics and Values: Ensuring that a Superintelligent AI shares our ethical values is a significant challenge. It is not just about programming the AI with a list of rules; it is about ensuring the AI understands and values these principles.

Power Concentration: Superintelligent AI could lead to an extreme concentration of power. Whoever controls the AI could potentially control everything else.

Economic Displacement: While AI could lead to new jobs and industries, it could also render many current jobs obsolete, leading to economic displacement on a massive scale.

In conclusion, while the realization of Superintelligent AI could be a watershed moment for humanity, it is also a development that we need to approach with utmost caution. We must ensure that research in this field is accompanied by rigorous safety and ethical considerations, and international dialogue about its implications is crucial.

1.4 Epilogue

Congratulations on completing the first step in your AI journey. By now you have gained a comprehensive overview of what AI is and its various types. With this foundational knowledge, you are now well-equipped to explore the major components of AI, which is the focus of our next chapter.

As you navigate the rest of this book, remember that understanding AI is not a destination, but a journey. It is about asking questions, seeking answers, and persisting in your quest for knowledge. So keep the curiosity alive and let's move forward to the next step.

CHAPTER 2: MAJOR COMPONENTS OF AI

Artificial Intelligence (AI) is a big and complex field that has many different parts and pieces that work together to make smart systems. In this chapter, we will look at five important parts: Machine Learning, Natural Language Processing, Robotics, Computer Vision, and Expert Systems. These parts are the main building blocks of AI, each adding something special to its abilities and skills. We will learn how these parts work together to make AI happen. As you read this chapter, keep in mind that each of these parts is (and potentially should be) a big area of study by itself. My goal here is to give you a general idea of how these parts make AI possible and what roles they play. Ready? Let's dive in!

2.1 Machine Learning

Machine learning is a subset of artificial intelligence and equips computers with the ability to learn and improve from experience without needing precise programming to do so.

Imagine teaching a child how to recognize a cat. You would show them many pictures of different cats. Over time, they would begin to understand the common features (like pointy ears, a tail, whiskers) that define a cat. They could then use this knowledge to identify a cat they have never seen before.

Machine learning works in a similar way. Let's take the same example - recognizing a cat. Instead of showing pictures to a child, we feed many pictures of cats to a computer algorithm (a machine learning model). The algorithm analyses these pictures and learns the features that define a cat. Once trained, the model can then recognize cats in new pictures it has never seen before.

In a nutshell, machine learning is all about training algorithms (or models) on data so that these algorithms can make accurate predictions or decisions without being specifically programmed to perform the task. It is like teaching a computer to make insightful decisions by learning from data.

There are three different types of machine learning (please note that we will be taking a much more detailed look at them in chapter four). They are:

- **Supervised Learning:** Here, the algorithm is schooled on labeled data, meaning that the datasets presented to the computer in the training process already have the desired categories defined. Once it has been trained on a specific dataset, it can extrapolate its learned knowledge to new, unseen data.

- **Unsupervised Learning:** This involves the algorithm learning from unlabeled data. It is responsible for identifying patterns and relationships within the data itself.

- **Reinforcement Learning**: This type of learning is based on a system of rewards or penalties. The algorithm improves its performance by interacting with its environment and adjusting its actions based on the feedback received.

2.2 Natural Language Processing

Natural Language Processing (NLP) is a fascinating field and subsection of the broad umbrella term of AI, focusing on the interaction between computers and humans through language. It aims to enable machines to understand, interpret, and generate human language in a valuable and meaningful way. NLP is a cornerstone technology for generative AI, providing the essential mechanism to comprehend textual prompts from users and transform them into creative outputs, based on the specific generative AI tool employed. This process encompasses several complex tasks, including language understanding, language generation, translation, and speech recognition.

Important NLP Tasks

- **Language Understanding**: NLP enables machines to understand the semantics and context of sentences, including the ability to understand idioms, metaphors, and other elements of everyday language. It even considers nuances such as tone, mood, and dialects. This is what allows a machine to derive the intended meaning from a sentence that could have different interpretations.

- **Language Generation**: Not only can NLP understand language, but it can also generate it. For instance, it can generate human-like text that mimics our writing style, maintains context, and stays coherent over several paragraphs. This is the core technology behind many AI writing assistants and chatbots.

- **Translation**: NLP powers translation tools that can convert text from one language to another, taking into account grammar rules and language nuances. This process involves understanding the source language and intelligently reproducing its meaning in the target language.

- **Speech Recognition**: While technically a separate field called Automatic Speech Recognition (ASR), speech recognition frequently intersects with NLP. It involves transcribing spoken language into written text, and is the key technology behind virtual assistants like Amazon's Alexa and Apple's Siri.

Let's dive in greater detail into...

Applications of NLP

- **Chatbots**: NLP plays a crucial role in powering chatbots, enabling them to comprehend and respond to text inputs from users. This functionality is crucial across sectors, offering customer support, product recommendations, personal assistant services, and more. For instance, a customer support chatbot might use NLP to understand a complaint or query and provide a helpful response.

- **Machine Translation**: Services such as Google Translate use NLP at their core to translate text from one language to another, making it easier for people across the globe to communicate and access information regardless of language barriers.

- **Sentiment Analysis**: Also known as opinion mining, sentiment analysis is a popular application of NLP. It involves using algorithms to determine the sentiment behind a piece of text. For example, these algorithms can scan through customer reviews, social media posts, or any text data to extract opinions and feelings, classifying them as positive, negative, or neutral. Businesses can use this information to understand customer opinions about a product or a service.).

In sum, NLP is a captivating AI discipline that helps bridge the communication gap between humans and machines, empowering computers to understand and replicate human language more effectively. It is one of the critical driving forces behind the exciting advancements we see in generative AI.

2.3 Robotics

Robotics, a branch of artificial intelligence, is an exciting and rapidly evolving field that focuses on creating and manipulating machines - robots, to perform tasks typically done by humans. The underlying goal of robotics is to design intelligent machines that can help and assist humans in their activities and in places that are inaccessible or dangerous, enhancing our capabilities and improving safety.

The breadth of robotics extends from simple, routine tasks to complex, intricate systems. At one end of the spectrum, we have robots like the Roomba vacuum cleaner that autonomously cleans your home, requiring minimal human intervention. On the other end, we have sophisticated systems such as self-driving cars, humanoid robots, and even surgical robots that perform complex medical procedures with precision.

Let's explore the...

Subfields of Robotics

- **Autonomous Vehicles:** Also known as self-driving cars, these are vehicles equipped with AI systems that can sense their environment and navigate without any human intervention. These vehicles utilize a combination of various technologies such as machine learning, computer vision, and sensor fusion to make decisions about their paths, speed, and whether to stop or slow down based on their surroundings. They also have to predict and respond to the actions of other drivers, pedestrians, and cyclists. Autonomous vehicles hold the promise of reducing road accidents, increasing fuel efficiency, and revolutionizing the transportation industry.

- **Humanoid Robots:** These are robots designed to mimic the human body and imitate human actions. The goal of humanoid robots is to create a machine that can operate in environments built for humans, use human tools, and interact with humans in a more natural manner. Humanoid robots can walk, talk, and even express emotions to some extent. A famous example is Sophia, a humanoid robot developed by Hanson Robotics, known for her advanced ability to communicate and make facial expressions.

Other areas of robotics include:

- **Industrial Robots:** These are robots used in manufacturing processes, including assembly, packaging, painting, and inspection. They perform repetitive, hazardous, or precise tasks more efficiently and consistently than humans.

- **Medical Robotics:** Robots in healthcare can perform precise surgeries, assist in patient care, rehabilitation, and dispense medication. A well-known example is the da Vinci Surgical System, which allows surgeons to perform minimally invasive surgeries with a high degree of precision.

- **Space Robotics:** Space robots, such as rovers and satellites, help explore planets, moons, and asteroids. They can withstand harsh environments and send valuable data back to Earth.

In conclusion, robotics, as an integral component of AI, has the potential to transform various aspects of our lives, industries, and explore realms beyond human reach. It demonstrates the incredible possibilities that lie at the intersection of artificial intelligence, mechanical engineering, and computer science.

2.4 Computer Vision

Computer vision is a field of artificial intelligence that trains computers to interpret and understand the visual world around them. It is all about teaching machines to "see" and interpret images, videos, and their surroundings in the same way that humans do. Through the use of digital images, computer vision systems can accurately identify and classify objects, and then react to what they "see."

Let's dive a little deeper into this concept and its subfields:

- **Image Recognition**: This is one of the most common and widely known applications of computer vision. It involves teaching machines to identify and classify objects, scenes, activities, and people in images and videos. For instance, social media platforms use image recognition to detect and tag faces in photos. In healthcare, it can be used to analyze medical images like MRIs or X-rays to detect diseases. In retail, image recognition can be used for surveillance, tracking customer behavior, and managing inventory.

- **Object Detection**: While image recognition can identify what objects are in an image, object detection goes a step further by locating the presence of objects in an image and placing a "bounding box" around them. This is particularly useful in self-driving cars where it is not just important to identify pedestrians or other vehicles but also to understand their location in relation to the vehicle.

- **Scene Understanding**: This is about analyzing the entire scene in an image, not just individual objects. It involves understanding the context of the objects, their relationship with each other, and the overall setting. This ability is crucial in fields like robotics and autonomous vehicles, where machines need to navigate through their environment.

- **Image Restoration**: This aspect of computer vision focuses on improving the quality of images and removing distortions. It is used in applications like photo restoration, enhancing satellite images, or in healthcare to improve the clarity of medical images.

- **Autonomous Vehicles**: One of the most advanced uses of computer vision is in self-driving cars. These vehicles use computer vision, along with other AI technologies, to interpret their surroundings, detect and avoid obstacles, read traffic signs, and make decisions about steering, acceleration, and braking.

- **Security and Surveillance**: Computer vision is used extensively in video surveillance to monitor spaces for unusual activity, crowd behavior, or individuals' actions. It can identify suspicious behaviors, track individuals across cameras, and even detect unattended objects.

In essence, computer vision is a key building block in developing intelligent systems that can perceive, understand, and navigate the world. This field is growing rapidly, making significant strides in areas such as facial recognition, disease detection, autonomous vehicles, and much more. Its applications are transforming industries and enhancing our ability to automate tasks, make accurate predictions, and gain insights from the visual data that surrounds us.

2.5 Expert Systems

Expert Systems are a significant element of artificial intelligence, designed to emulate the decision-making skills of a human expert. They are configured to solve complex problems by reasoning with knowledge that is often presented as "if-then" rules, rather than the traditional procedural code. By simulating the judgment and behavior of an expert in a particular field, Expert Systems can make informed decisions, offer advice, or recommend actions.

Let us delve deeper into the nature of Expert Systems:

- **Knowledge Base**: The knowledge base is the cornerstone of an Expert System. This is where the system stores the detailed information it uses to make decisions. The data within the knowledge base is usually gathered from human experts and is organized as a set of rules or a network of interconnected facts.

- **Inference Engine**: This component is the reasoning powerhouse of an Expert System. The Inference Engine applies logical operations to infer new knowledge from the stored facts and rules in the knowledge base. It emulates the problem-solving and decision-making skills of human experts, using a systematic, step-by-step approach to derive conclusions.

- **User Interface**: Expert Systems interact with users through a user-friendly interface. Here, users input queries or problems, and the system provides corresponding solutions or suggestions based on its knowledge base and inference engine.

Applications of Expert Systems

Expert Systems have diverse applications across several fields. Below are some notable instances:

- **Medical Diagnosis**: Expert Systems can assist doctors in diagnosing diseases. They process the symptoms provided by the physician, comparing these symptoms with a database of known diseases and their corresponding symptoms. These systems can also suggest a treatment plan based on the diagnosed disease, thereby enhancing patient care.

- **Financial Services**: In the financial industry, Expert Systems are valuable assets. They can automate and enhance decision-making processes, such as loan approvals or investment portfolio management.

An Expert System, for example, can assess the creditworthiness of a loan applicant by comparing their financial and personal data against predefined criteria. Similarly, they can suggest investment strategies based on an investor's risk profile, financial goals, and market trends.

- **Other Industries**: Besides healthcare and finance, Expert Systems are being employed in various other fields. They are used in weather forecasting, geological exploration, and software development, among other areas. In the field of education, they have been used to create intelligent tutoring systems.

In conclusion, Expert Systems leverage the depth and breadth of human expertise, making it accessible and applicable across various domains. By combining the efficiency and scalability of computers with the knowledge of human experts, Expert Systems exemplify the transformative power of AI.

2.6 Major Components of AI - Epilogue

With the close of this chapter, you now have an understanding of the major components of AI. You have seen how Machine Learning gives machines the ability to learn, how Natural Language Processing makes machines understand and generate human language, how Computer Vision equips machines with the ability to interpret visual data, how Robotics enables machines to interact with the physical world, and how Expert Systems empower machines to emulate the decision-making ability of human experts.

These components act together to construct intelligent systems capable of tasks that were once considered exclusive to humans. As we progress, we'll explore how these components find their practical application in various domains and form the foundation for Generative AI.

CHAPTER 3: BASIC PRINCIPLES OF AI

In this chapter, we will look at the basic principles that make AI work. These basic principles are the role of data and understanding algorithms. Data is the information that AI uses to learn and make decisions. Algorithms are the rules that AI follows to process data and learn from it. You will learn how data and algorithms are essential for AI and how they work together to make AI happen.

Be sure to complete this entire chapter (and feel free to go back to it), as it serves as an important foundation for the next two chapters, in which we are going to be discussing the different types of machine learning and deep learning methods.

3.1 The Role of Data in AI

The enormous progress that recent years have brought for AI research and practice can be largely attributed to the increasing availability of high-quality data. Data acts as the backbone of AI, providing the 'experience' from which AI systems learn. The type, quality, and volume of data are vital factors in determining the performance of AI systems.

3.1.1 Training Data: The Foundation of AI Learning

Training data are the pivotal learning materials for AI systems. They serve as the core resource from which these systems gain their knowledge and hone their skills. We'll go into more detail about the nature of training data, its significance, and the influence of its quality and quantity on the performance of an AI system.

- **Nature of Training Data:** Consider training data as the tutor of an AI system. It comes in the form of a dataset that includes pairs of input data and their corresponding outputs. These data pairs provide the problem scenarios (inputs) and their respective solutions (outputs) for the AI to learn from. Imagine a child learning math; the child is given a math problem (the input) and the solution (the output). By working through many problems and their solutions, the child starts to understand the logic behind solving such problems. Similarly, these pairs of input-output teach the AI how to recognize patterns, make connections, and ultimately, make accurate predictions or decisions based on new, unseen input data.

- **Importance of Quality:** High-quality training data is like having an excellent teacher; it is a critical factor for a successful learning experience. When we talk about 'quality', we're referring to data that is accurate, relevant to the problem at hand, and unbiased. It is important to understand that AI systems are only as good as the data they learn from. If the training data is flawed with errors, contains irrelevant information, or is biased in some way, the AI system could learn incorrect patterns. This can result in the system making incorrect predictions or decisions when it is used in real-world scenarios. In other words, inaccurate training data can lead to inaccurate AI behavior, much like a student being misguided by incorrect teaching.

- **Impact of Quantity:** The amount of training data used in AI is another key aspect that can significantly influence an AI system's performance. Generally, the more data the system has to learn from, the better it can understand the complexity of the problem and make accurate predictions. The reason is simple: larger datasets offer a more comprehensive representation of the scenario or problem the AI needs to solve. However, the relationship between data quantity and model performance is not linear or straightforward. The nature of the task at hand also plays a role. For simpler tasks, a smaller dataset of high quality might be enough to train the AI effectively. On the other hand, for more complex tasks like image recognition or natural language processing, a large amount of high-quality data would be required for the AI to perform well.

3.1.2 Real-world Data: The Messiness and Value

Real-world data is the cornerstone of developing AI systems that perform well in practical, everyday situations. As the name suggests, this is data that comes directly from the world around us, and as such, it can be messy and complex. Dealing with this data requires careful handling and preprocessing, and in this section, we will explore the vital steps of data cleaning and data transformation.

The Nature of Real-world Data

Before diving into the preprocessing steps, it is important to understand the nature of real-world data. This is data that hasn't been sanitized or arranged neatly in rows and columns for easy analysis. It might come from social media posts, customer reviews, sensor readings, audio recordings, or any number of other sources. It often includes a mix of data types, such as text, numbers, dates, and more. Furthermore, real-world data can be incomplete, inconsistent, or contain outright errors. Despite these challenges, real-world data is invaluable for AI systems because it reflects the complexity and diversity of the situations these systems will encounter in practice.

Data Cleaning: Making Sense of the Mess

The first step in dealing with real-world data usually needs to be what is referred to as "data cleaning", the process of detecting and correcting or removing errors and inconsistencies from the existing data. Data cleaning might involve tasks like correcting spelling errors, dealing with missing or incomplete data, removing duplicate entries, and checking for and handling outliers (values that are significantly different from the others).

For example, consider an AI system that is being trained to analyse customer reviews. The raw data might include reviews with spelling errors, missing ratings, or duplicate entries. A data cleaning process would be needed to ensure that these issues don't distort the AI's understanding of the data.

Data Transformation: Adapting Data for AI Algorithms

Once the data has been cleaned, it often needs to be transformed so AI algorithms can actually use it. This process is called data transformation, and it can include several different steps:

- **Normalization**: This is the process of scaling numeric data to fit within a specific range, such as between 0 and 1, or a standard deviation from a mean value. Normalization helps ensure that all the features (input variables) contribute equally to the AI's learning process, preventing any single feature from dominating simply because of its scale.

- **Discretization**: This involves converting continuous data into discrete categories. For example, an AI system might need to categorize people's ages into groups (like "child," "teenager," "adult," "senior") rather than dealing with each individual age.

- **Encoding**: In this process, categorical data, such as "yes" and "no" responses or different types of products, are transformed into a numeric format that can be used by AI algorithms. For example, an encoding process might convert "yes" responses to 1 and "no" responses to 0.

By carefully cleaning and transforming real-world data, we can help ensure that our AI systems are learning from the best data possible and are well-prepared to handle real-world tasks.

3.1.3 Big Data: The Fuel for Advanced AI

In the exciting and fast-evolving world of AI, 'big data' is a term you'll frequently encounter. It refers to datasets of such colossal size and complexity that they cannot be effectively managed, processed, or analyzed with traditional data processing software. The emergence of big data has been a key driver in the rapid advancements we've seen in AI, particularly in the field of machine learning.

Unpacking the 3Vs of Big Data

In understanding big data, three aspects are crucial: volume, velocity, and variety, often collectively referred to as the 3Vs of big data.

- **Volume**: This simply refers to the sheer size of these datasets. We're talking about quantities that can range from terabytes (equivalent to thousands of gigabytes) to zettabytes (equivalent to a billion terabytes) and beyond. These huge volumes of data can provide a treasure trove of information for AI systems to learn from.

- **Velocity**: This term refers to the speed at which new data is being generated and collected. In today's hyperconnected world, data is being created at an unprecedented rate — from social media posts, to e-commerce transactions, to IoT device readings and more. The faster new data comes in, the more rapidly an AI system can learn and adapt.

- **Variety**: In the context of big data, variety refers to the different types of data that are now available. These can range from structured data (like spreadsheets with clear rows and columns) to unstructured data (like text, images, videos, social media posts, and sensor data). The wide variety of data types presents both challenges and opportunities for AI systems, enabling them to learn from a richer tapestry of human and machine activity.

Big Data's Role in Machine Learning

Big data has had a transformative impact on machine learning, a key subset of AI. Machine learning models excel at finding patterns in data. The more data they have to learn from, the better they can become at predicting outcomes, making decisions, and understanding complex relationships. This is particularly true for a type of machine learning called deep learning.

Deep learning models use artificial neural networks with multiple layers (hence "deep") to model high-level abstractions in data. These models can handle vast amounts of input data and identify complex patterns. However, they need a lot of data to learn effectively. Here's where big data comes into play: it provides the vast quantities of data needed to train these models. Thanks to big data, deep learning models can excel in tasks like image and speech recognition, natural language processing, and many others.

By harnessing the power of big data, we can build AI systems that are more sophisticated, more accurate, and more useful than ever before. With more data being created every day, the potential for future advancements in AI is virtually limitless.

3.2 Understanding Algorithms in AI

Algorithms are at the heart of Artificial Intelligence (AI), guiding systems to learn, adapt, and make intelligent decisions. In this chapter, 'Understanding the Importance of Algorithms in AI,' we delve into the fundamental properties, significance, and diverse applications of these essential AI components.

From their role in optimization and automation to their usage in data processing and machine learning, we shed light on the omnipresence of algorithms in AI. We further explore their types categorized under supervised, unsupervised, and reinforcement learning, alongside a deep dive into specific machine learning algorithms like linear regression, decision trees, and neural networks.

Let's demystify the world of AI algorithms and learn about their indispensable role in shaping intelligent behavior in AI systems.

3.2.1 Deeper into the Nature of Algorithms

Before you can fully understand the complexity and the elegance of algorithms, we first have to cover their fundamental properties – all algorithms must be deterministic, terminating and feasible.

- **Deterministic:** An algorithm is deterministic, meaning that for a given input, it will always produce the same output. This predictability is what makes algorithms reliable and effective in problem-solving and data processing tasks.

- **Terminating:** A valid algorithm must eventually come to an end. Whether it is reaching a solution or simply exhausting all possible avenues, an algorithm can't go on indefinitely.

- **Feasible:** An algorithm needs to be practical, and its steps need to be achievable using the resources available. This is especially important when dealing with large datasets or complex computations in AI.

3.2.2 The Undeniable Importance of Algorithms

The role of algorithms in the digital age extends beyond just computation, they serve essential functions in optimizing business workflows and decision-making, to automate tasks in business and manufacturing and are at the heart of more and more innovation.

- **Optimization:** Algorithms, especially in AI, are used to optimize processes and tasks, finding the most efficient or effective ways of doing things. This includes optimizing resource allocation, improving decision-making, and even optimizing machine learning models themselves.

- **Automation:** Algorithms are at the heart of automation, allowing tasks to be carried out automatically without the need for human intervention. This automation extends from simple tasks, such as data sorting, to complex tasks like driving autonomous vehicles.

- **Innovation:** By enabling new ways of processing and interpreting data, algorithms drive innovation in many fields. In AI, this has led to breakthroughs in areas such as natural language processing, computer vision, and reinforcement learning.

3.2.3 A Closer Look at Algorithms' Applications in AI

From simple tasks to complex machine learning, algorithms power every aspect of AI.

- **Data Processing**: Basic algorithms are used to clean and pre-process data, preparing it for further analysis. This includes tasks like handling missing data, removing duplicates, and normalizing variables.

- **Machine Learning:** Algorithms form the backbone of all machine learning models. Whether it is a simple linear regression or a complex deep learning model, an algorithm is what allows the model to learn from data and make predictions or decisions.

- **Deep Learning:** More complex algorithms, such as artificial neural networks, are the driving force behind deep learning. These algorithms enable machines to learn from vast amounts of data and carry out tasks that were previously thought to be the exclusive domain of humans, such as recognizing images and understanding natural language.

In essence, understanding the nature, significance, and applications of algorithms is fundamental to comprehending the inner workings of AI.

3.2.4 Purpose and Types of AI Algorithms

When we talk about AI algorithms, we typically group them into three main categories: supervised learning algorithms, unsupervised learning algorithms, and reinforcement learning algorithms. We'll delve into each of these, offering some easy-to-understand examples.

3.2.4.1 Supervised Learning Algorithms: Predicting Outcomes

Supervised learning is a crucial part of machine learning and it's all about making educated predictions based on data that has already been labelled manually.

- **Linear Regression:** Think of this as an algorithm that helps us guess future values based on past trends. For instance, if we know the size, location, and age of several houses along with their prices, linear regression helps us predict how much a new house might cost based on these features. It does this by finding the best-fitting line, known as the regression line, that represents the relationship between these factors (or variables).

- **Logistic Regression:** Despite having 'regression' in its name, this is actually about classifying things into categories. For instance, it could be used to decide whether an email is spam (labeled as 1) or not spam (labeled as 0) based on the email's content, sender, and so on.

- **Support Vector Machines:** SVM is a versatile algorithm used for categorizing things, even when the categories aren't easily separated. This could be classifying emails as 'business' or 'personal', even when there's a lot of overlap between the two. It works by finding a boundary (the hyperplane) that best divides the categories based on the data.

3.2.4.2 Unsupervised Learning Algorithms: Finding Patterns

Unsupervised learning is about understanding, structuring, and extracting meaningful information from unlabeled data.

- **K-means Clustering:** Imagine you're a librarian with a pile of books that haven't been sorted by genre. K-means clustering is an algorithm that helps you sort these books into distinct groups based on common attributes like book title, author, or even the first sentence. Similarly, this algorithm can help businesses understand their customers better by grouping them based on their purchasing behaviors.

- **Principal Component Analysis (PCA):** Sometimes, we have more data than we know what to do with. PCA is a technique that reduces this data to a manageable size, while keeping its important structure and relationships intact. It's like summarizing a lengthy book into a few key points that still capture the essence of the story.

3.2.4.3 Reinforcement Learning Algorithms: Learning by Doing

Reinforcement learning is about taking suitable action to maximize reward in a particular situation. It is employed by various software and machines to find the best possible behavior or path it should take in a specific context.

- **Q-learning:** It's a strategy-free reinforcement learning algorithm. Imagine teaching a robot to navigate a maze. The robot tries different paths (actions), and each time it hits a dead-end or finds the exit, it learns more about the maze (current state). Over time, the robot learns the most efficient way to navigate the maze.

- **Deep Q Network (DQN):** This is an advanced form of Q-learning that works well with more complex problems. It combines Q-learning with deep neural networks to handle large and complicated situations, like playing video games at superhuman levels.

Remember, every algorithm has its strengths and weaknesses, and the trick to effective AI is choosing the best-suited algorithm for your specific task.

3.2.5 Exploring Specific Machine Learning Algorithms

In this section, we're going to explore three important machine learning algorithms: Linear Regression, Decision Trees, and Neural Networks. We'll break down what they do and how they work in a simple, understandable way.

3.2.5.1 Linear Regression: The Foundation of Predictive Analysis

Linear regression is a basic, yet powerful tool used mostly for making predictions. It's like trying to draw a straight line through a scatter plot of data points that best represents the relationship between two variables.

Imagine you're trying to guess the price of a house based on its size. The size of the house (the independent variable) and the price of the house (the dependent variable) have a relationship that linear regression tries to capture. By drawing a line of best fit through your data, you can use it to make educated guesses about future house prices based on their sizes. However, remember that linear regression assumes that everything in the world follows a straight line, which is not always the case in real life.

3.2.5.2 Decision Trees: Making Decisions, Step by Step

Decision trees are straightforward and easy-to-understand algorithms. They help you make decisions by dividing data into smaller groups and making a decision tree that visually represents these groups and their outcomes.

Think of decision trees like a game of 20 questions. For instance, you're trying to decide if someone should be given a loan. The decision tree takes into account factors like their income, job stability, and credit history, splitting people into different categories based on these variables. At the end of the tree, you're left with a series of decisions leading to an outcome: should the person get a loan or not?

3.2.5.3 Neural Networks: Mimicking the Human Brain

Neural networks are the workhorses behind deep learning, loosely emulating how our brains work to learn from heaps of data. Even a simple, one-layered neural network can generate basic predictions, but by adding more layers, we can refine these predictions.

A neural network is made of nodes (like brain cells) connected by layers (like synapses). Each node holds a value, which could be an input or an output, and connections between these nodes allow information to flow from one to another.

For example, neural networks have made breakthroughs in computer vision, a field that teaches machines to 'see' like us. By processing pixels from images as inputs, the neural network can learn to identify patterns and shapes, enabling technologies like facial recognition and self-driving cars.

With these simplified explanations, you should have a clearer picture of these machine learning algorithms and their role in powering AI systems.

3.3 Basic Principles of AI - Epilogue

By now, you should have a deeper understanding of the foundational principles that guide AI: the significant role data plays and the intricate workings of algorithms. These principles are the lifeblood of AI, driving its learning and decision-making capabilities. As we move forward, we will build on these fundamental concepts, diving into specific areas of AI, such as Machine Learning, and its types. Keep these principles in mind as they will continually resurface, underpinning everything you learn about AI.

CHAPTER 4: MACHINE LEARNING AND ITS TYPES

With a solid understanding of the foundational principles of AI, we will now turn our attention to a crucial subset of AI - Machine Learning (ML). At its core, ML is about teaching machines to learn from experience, much like humans do, but with far greater scale and speed. In this chapter, we explore the three main types of machine learning: Supervised Learning, Unsupervised Learning, and Reinforcement Learning (remember the three different types of algorithms from the previous chapter!?).

Each of these types offers a different approach to learning, making them suited for distinct kinds of problems. By the end of this chapter, you will have a firm grasp of the principles of machine learning and its types, an important understanding that will also help you to better make sense of and use the generative AI tools we will cover in the second section of this book.

4.1 Supervised Learning: Learning from Labeled Data

In the realm of machine learning, supervised learning holds a prominent position due to its efficiency and widespread use. It is called 'supervised' because the process of learning in this paradigm closely resembles the way a student learns under the guidance of a teacher. The 'teacher', in this case, is a dataset containing inputs and their corresponding correct outputs — also known as labels.

4.1.1 The Mechanism of Supervised Learning

In supervised learning, the learning algorithm is provided with a set of example pairs consisting of an input object (typically a vector) and a desired output value (the label). The algorithm analyzes the training data and produces an inferred function, which can be used for mapping new instances.

The quality of the output, or the predictions made by the model, is measured against a predetermined set of measures called a cost function or loss function. This function indicates the degree of disparity between the predicted and the actual output, and the aim is to minimize this cost function.

4.1.2 Types of Supervised Learning

There are two primary types of supervised learning tasks: regression and classification. In regression tasks, the output is a continuous variable, such as a house price or a person's age. Linear regression and polynomial regression are examples of algorithms used for these tasks.

On the other hand, classification tasks involve predicting a discrete class label output such as spam or not-spam for emails. Algorithms used for classification tasks include logistic regression, support vector machines, k-nearest neighbours, and decision trees, among others.

4.1.3 Applications of Supervised Learning

Supervised learning is applied in all kinds of industries. For instance, in the healthcare sector, it is used to predict whether a patient has a certain disease based on their symptoms. In finance, supervised learning can determine the creditworthiness of a loan applicant. It is also extensively used in the technology industry for applications like voice recognition, facial recognition, and even spam detection in emails.

Basically, supervised learning is always the go-to-method in tasks where patterns in existing data can predict outcomes in new data. Despite its power and flexibility, supervised learning is not without its challenges. It requires a substantial amount of labelled data, and the quality of the output strongly depends on the quality of the input data. Moreover, the challenge of overfitting, where the model performs well on the training data but poorly on unseen data, is also a crucial issue that has to be overcome.

4.2 Unsupervised Learning: Identifying Hidden Patterns

Unsupervised learning stands as a different yet equally powerful method of learning compared to supervised learning. In unsupervised learning, the algorithm deals with unlabeled data and thus lacks a clear-cut guide or 'supervisor.' It is tasked with finding structure, relationships, or meaningful insights directly from the input data, making it a form of self-discovery.

4.2.1 Mechanism of Unsupervised Learning

Without prior knowledge of what constitutes a correct or incorrect outcome, unsupervised learning algorithms must develop their own understanding of the data. They work by analyzing the structure and distribution of the data, often identifying groups or patterns that might not be immediately obvious.

They essentially look for data instances that are similar and group them together, thereby forming various clusters within the data. In doing so, they can unveil hidden relationships, underlying patterns, or intrinsic groupings that may not have been obvious at first glance.

4.2.2 Types of Unsupervised Learning

The two primary categories of unsupervised learning are clustering and dimensionality reduction. Clustering algorithms, such as K-means, hierarchical clustering, and DBSCAN, group similar instances together. These algorithms can find the natural groupings in data or identify unusual data points (outliers).

Dimensionality reduction techniques, like Principal Component Analysis (PCA), Singular Value Decomposition (SVD), or t-SNE, aim to simplify the data without losing too much information. They are used to merge or drop variables in a dataset, making the data easier to explore and visualize.

4.2.3 Applications of Unsupervised Learning

Unsupervised learning has wide-ranging applications, including but not limited to anomaly detection, clustering, and data pre-processing.

In the realm of cybersecurity, anomaly detection can identify unusual patterns or behaviors that could signify a network intrusion. Applied in a marketing context, unsupervised learning techniques are used to identify different customer segments or demographics based on purchasing behavior, allowing businesses to target their marketing efforts more effectively.

Despite its many applications, unsupervised learning comes with a number of challenges. The most notable one is that its outcomes can be unpredictable and difficult to validate due to the lack of a 'ground truth.' Consequently, data analysts and researchers must carefully interpret and analyse the outcomes of the algorithm to ensure its quality.

4.3 Reinforcement Learning: Learning through Trial and Error

Reinforcement Learning (RL) is a special branch of machine learning. Unlike other types where learning comes from a predefined dataset, reinforcement learning is all about learning by doing. It interacts with its surroundings, receiving positive or negative feedback (rewards or penalties) and adjusting its actions accordingly, with the ultimate goal of maximizing its overall reward in the long run.

4.3.1 Basic Principles of Reinforcement Learning

Think of reinforcement learning as a loop of trial and error. An RL "agent" (the learner) performs an action in an environment. This action leads the environment to a new state, and the agent gets either a reward or a penalty. The agent's job is to figure out a "policy", a rule that helps it decide what actions to take in different situations to gather the maximum sum of rewards over time.

However, it's not as simple as just chasing immediate rewards. The agent's actions influence future rewards too, so it must weigh the long-term implications of its actions. This so-called "problem of delayed rewards" adds to the complexity of reinforcement learning.

4.3.2 Key Components of Reinforcement Learning

Let's break down the key parts of a RL system. There's an agent, which is the learner and decision-maker. The environment is everything the agent interacts with and can affect the agent's state. States are specific situations the agent finds itself in, and actions are the choices it can make. The reward is feedback that the agent uses to gauge if its actions were successful.

The entire reinforcement learning process is typically mapped out as a Markov Decision Process (MDP), a mathematical model used for decision-making scenarios where outcomes are partly due to chance and partly due to the agent's actions.

4.3.3 Applications of Reinforcement Learning

Reinforcement learning has had impressive impacts in various fields. For instance, in gaming, a program developed by DeepMind named AlphaGo, used RL to beat world champions in the complex game of Go.

In robotics, RL allows robots to learn sophisticated tasks like balancing or manipulating objects using raw sensor inputs. It's also becoming popular for personalizing recommendations in digital advertising and optimizing dynamic pricing in online shopping.

Despite these advancements, reinforcement learning does have its obstacles. It often requires a lot of data and computation power. Striking the right balance between exploration (testing new actions) and exploitation (sticking with proven actions) is another key challenge in RL.

While reinforcement learning holds great potential, it's not a fix-all solution. The decision to use RL or another type of learning (like supervised or unsupervised learning) will depend on the specific problem and the resources available.

4.4 Machine Learning and its Types - Epilogue

By completing this chapter, you have gained an essential understanding of Machine Learning and its various types. You have seen how Supervised Learning enables machines to learn from labeled data, how Unsupervised Learning allows machines to identify hidden patterns, and how Reinforcement Learning lets machines learn through trial and error. These learning methods form the backbone of many AI systems you'll encounter in the real world. As we move forward, you will see these principles take form in more complex structures like Neural Networks and Deep Learning.

CHAPTER 5: NEURAL NETWORKS AND DEEP LEARNING

Now that you have a solid understanding of Machine Learning, we are now going to venture into the fascinating world of Neural Networks and Deep Learning. These advanced concepts build on the principles of machine learning, adding depth and complexity to create even more powerful AI models.

This chapter introduces you to the concept of Artificial Neural Networks, a computational model inspired by the human brain's structure.

We will then explore Deep Learning, a field of study that employs these networks at a large scale to recognize complex patterns in data. Along this journey, we will also delve into the specifics of Convolutional Neural Networks and Recurrent Neural Networks. Be prepared for a deep dive into the cutting-edge techniques that are transforming the face of AI.

Neural networks and deep learning have become pillars of AI, responsible for some of the most impressive advancements in the field in recent years.

5.1 Artificial Neural Networks: Mimicking the Human Brain

Artificial Neural Networks (ANNs) draw inspiration from biological neural networks, specifically the ones found in the human brain. Inspired by their design, the goal for ANNs is to recreate the capability of brains to recognize patterns and solve complex problems.

5.1.1 Structure of an Artificial Neural Network

Artificial Neural Networks (ANNs) are like an attempt to replicate the human brain in a simplified way. They're made up of units called "neurons" or nodes that are arranged in different layers. These nodes are linked together, allowing information to flow from one to the other. Generally, an ANN consists of three main layers:

- Input Layer: As the name suggests, this layer takes in the input data. The nodes here match the number of features or data points in the input dataset.

- Hidden Layer(s): These are the layers sandwiched between the input and output layers. They process the information received from the preceding layer and pass the processed information to the following layer. How complex an ANN is usually depends on the number of hidden layers and the number of neurons in each hidden layer.

- Output Layer: This layer generates the final outcome or decision. The number of nodes here is usually tied to the number of possible output classes or values.

5.1.2 Functioning of a Neuron

Each neuron in an ANN is a computational unit that performs a specific function. The neuron receives one or more inputs, applies a weight to each input, sums up the weighted inputs, and then applies an activation function to the sum to generate an output.

The weights are parameters that the network learns during the training phase. The activation function determines the output of a neuron given its inputs. Some common activation functions include the sigmoid function, the hyperbolic tangent function, and the Rectified Linear Unit (ReLU) function.

5.1.3 Learning in Artificial Neural Networks

The main goal of an ANN is to learn from data, a process that occurs during its training. The network gets training data and adjusts the weights of its neurons through a method called backpropagation.

Backpropagation is a technique used in ANNs to tweak the weights of neurons. The aim is to minimize the difference between the network's predicted output and the actual output. To this end a unique method called "gradient descent" is used – in that method, the weights are progressively adjusted to lower the error function.

After the network is trained, it can predict outputs for new inputs it hasn't seen before. That's why ANNs are so useful in tasks like image recognition, understanding natural language, and predictive modeling.

5.2 Deep Learning: Harnessing the Power of Depth

Deep Learning is a subset of machine learning that's inspired by how the human brain works. It's designed to learn from a lot of data using artificial neural networks that have many layers, which is hence the term "deep".

5.2.1 The Depth of Deep Learning

The depth in deep learning comes from the number of layers in the artificial neural network. These layers are set up in a hierarchical order, with each layer learning to pull out specific features from the data it gets. As data moves through the layers, the network learns to recognize more complex features, allowing it to understand complicated data representations.

For example, in image recognition, the first few layers might only learn to detect edges or basic shapes. As you go deeper into the network, the layers could start identifying more complex features like objects, faces, or even entire scenes.

5.2.2 Training Deep Learning Models

Training deep learning models is about giving the model a lot of labeled data, letting it make predictions, and then adjusting the model's weights based on the mistakes it makes. This is done using a method called backpropagation, which starts from the last layer and works its way back, tweaking the weights to reduce the error in the output.

But, training deep learning models can be a hefty task because it involves a lot of parameters. That's why it typically needs high-performing hardware, often GPUs, and lots of data.

5.2.3 Applications of Deep Learning

Deep learning has shown remarkable results in various fields. Here are a few examples:

- **Image Recognition:** Deep learning models, especially Convolutional Neural Networks (CNNs), have done exceptionally well in image recognition tasks. They're used in facial recognition systems, diagnosing medical images, and in self-driving cars.

- **Speech Recognition:** Voice technologies like Google Assistant, Amazon's Alexa, and Apple's Siri are based on deep learning models. Recurrent Neural Networks (RNNs), a type of deep learning model, are usually used for this because they're good at handling sequential data.

- **Natural Language Processing:** The NLP field has also been revolutionized by deep learning, enabling applications like machine translation, text generation, and sentiment analysis. Here again, Recurrent Neural Networks and their variations (like LSTM and GRU) are commonly used due to their proficiency with sequence data.

- **Autonomous Vehicles:** Deep learning plays a vital role in developing self-driving cars. These vehicles use deep learning to understand their environment and make driving decisions, reducing the need for humans.

While deep learning is indeed powerful, it's not always the best tool for the job. The choice of model depends on the problem you're trying to solve, the data you have, and what you specifically need for the task.

5.3 Convolutional Neural Networks: Understanding Images

Convolutional Neural Networks (CNNs) are a type of deep learning model that is really good at dealing with data organized in a grid, like images. CNNs are great at tasks like recognizing images and videos, leading to many advancements in computer vision, which is about helping computers "see" and understand visual data like humans do.

5.3.1 CNN Architecture

A CNN is designed explicitly to process grid-like data. It's made up of a few types of layers:

- **Convolutional layers:** These layers apply a set of filters to the input data. Each filter is quite small compared to the input, but it scans across the entire input, letting the model detect patterns anywhere in the input. This leads to 'translation invariance', meaning the model can recognize a pattern no matter where it is in the image.

- **Pooling (or subsampling) layers:** Through pooling, this type of layer reduces the size of the input, simplifying the calculations the model has to do and making the output less sensitive to minor changes in the input.

- **Fully connected layers:** In the final step, fully connected layers are applied to do the "high-level thinking". They take the feature maps (processed inputs) from the previous layers and turn them into a single vector (a line of data) that the next layers can process.

5.3.2 How CNNs Learn

Like other deep learning models, CNNs learn through a process known as backpropagation. Initially, filters are just random values. As the model is trained, these values are updated to help the model better recognize patterns in the input.

Each filter in the convolutional layer is designed to detect a specific pattern. When these filters are applied to the input, they create feature maps, which are passed on to the next layers. This keeps happening until the final layer, typically a fully connected layer, which gives the final output, such as a label in an image classification task.

5.3.3 Applications of CNNs

CNNs have led to many big leaps in computer vision. Here are a few examples:

- **Image Classification:** A common use of CNNs is categorizing images into predefined groups. This can range from something simple like figuring out if a picture is of a cat or a dog, to something complex like identifying hundreds of different objects in one image.

- **Object Detection:** Object detection is about identifying what objects are in an image and also showing where each object is located. CNNs play a key part in this.

- **Facial Recognition:** CNNs are also important in facial recognition technology. They're used to identify people, detect facial features, and even figure out emotional states.

- **Semantic Segmentation:** This task is about labeling each pixel in an image with the class of the object or area it belongs to. This is helpful in many areas, including self-driving cars and medical imaging.

Through these uses and others, CNNs have greatly improved the field of computer vision and continue to be a big area of research and development.

5.4 Recurrent Neural Networks: Learning from Sequences

Recurrent Neural Networks (RNNs) are a unique kind of neural network designed for dealing with data that comes in sequences or has a time element. Because of their special design, they can use their internal memory to process sequences of inputs. This makes them great at handling data where timing and sequence are important.

5.4.1 Architecture of RNNs

RNNs are designed to make good use of sequential data. In a standard neural network, we assume that all inputs (and outputs) don't depend on each other. But for many tasks, this assumption doesn't really work. For example, if you want to predict the next word in a sentence, you really need to know what the previous words were. That's where RNNs come in.

Each neuron in an RNN has a self-loop with a specific weight, creating an internal state or memory. This lets it keep information from one step to the next. The output at any given time step depends not just on the input at that time step, but also on the 'context' captured by the network's internal state. This state summarizes the information from previous time steps.

5.4.2 How RNNs Process Sequential Data

RNNs handle sequential data by taking in one element of the sequence at each time step and updating their internal state based on both this element and the previous state. This lets them capture and use the time-related dependencies in the sequence.

However, traditional RNNs have trouble learning long-term dependencies because of an issue known as the vanishing gradient problem. More advanced types of RNNs, like Long Short-Term Memory (LSTM) networks and Gated

Recurrent Unit (GRU) networks, have ways to lessen this issue. This makes them better at learning from sequences with long-term dependencies.

5.4.3 Applications of RNNs

RNNs, especially the more advanced kinds, are used a lot in tasks involving sequential data. Here are a few examples:

- **Natural Language Processing (NLP):** RNNs are used for many NLP tasks like machine translation, text generation, and sentiment analysis. Their ability to handle sequences makes them great at working with sentences and documents.

- **Speech Recognition:** In this context, RNNs can be used to process audio data over time and convert spoken language into written text.

- **Time Series Analysis:** RNNs can model complex time-related dependencies in time-series data. This makes them useful for tasks like predicting stock prices or weather forecasting.

The type of neural network you choose depends on the task you're trying to accomplish and the nature of your data. While RNNs are powerful, they also have their limitations and challenges, like difficulty learning long-term dependencies and high computational requirements. Despite these challenges, their ability to handle sequential data has made them incredibly valuable in many areas of AI.

5.5 Neural Networks and Deep Learning - Epilogue

Congratulations on completing this important chapter. You should now have a good understanding of Neural Networks and Deep Learning. You've seen how these advanced AI models are capable of recognizing complex patterns and making powerful predictions. By understanding how Convolutional Neural Networks interpret images and how Recurrent Neural Networks learn from sequences, you've gained a deeper insight into the inner workings of AI. As we continue our journey, you'll see how these concepts apply to different fields of AI and underpin the operations of Generative AI.

CHAPTER 6: MAJOR FIELDS OF AI

Now that we've seen the principles and techniques that drive Artificial Intelligence, it is time to explore the major fields where these concepts are actually applied. In this chapter, we dive into Natural Language Processing, Computer Vision, and Robotics. These are areas where AI truly shines, demonstrating its capacity to understand human language, interpret visual information, and interact with the physical world. As we journey through each field, you will begin to appreciate how the principles and techniques you've learned so far come together to create powerful, practical AI systems.

6.1 Natural Language Processing: Making Computers Understand Human Language

Natural Language Processing (NLP) is a fascinating field that sits at the intersection of artificial intelligence, computer science, and linguistics. Its main goal? To teach computers how to understand, interpret, generate, and respond to human languages. Each task within NLP comes with its own set of challenges and methods.

6.1.1 Understanding and Generating Text: Key Tasks in NLP

NLP is all about understanding and creating language. Here are some of the main tasks it tackles:

6.1.1.1 Sentiment Analysis

Sentiment Analysis, sometimes called opinion mining, is about figuring out the emotions or subjective information hidden in written or spoken language. It's like reading between the lines to understand the speaker or writer's feelings, opinions, and attitudes about a particular topic, or to determine the overall emotional tone of a text.

Sentiment analysis has many uses and is especially handy for things like brand monitoring, making sense of customer feedback, and keeping an eye on public sentiment on social media. In the world of politics, it can be used to gauge public opinion about candidates or issues.

6.1.1.2 Text Classification

Text Classification is all about sorting text into different groups. Thanks to NLP, text classifiers can automatically analyze text and assign it to predefined tags or categories based on what the text is about.

Text classification is used in spam detection, news categorization, sentiment analysis, and much more. It also finds use in various applications such as streamlining CRM tasks, improving web browsing, and sorting personal email.

6.1.1.3 Machine Translation

Machine Translation (MT) is the complex task of automatically translating text from one human language to another. Despite its challenges, thanks to Neural Machine Translation (NMT), we've seen incredible progress. Systems today can translate between many languages, often achieving results similar to human translators.

6.1.1.4 Text Generation

Text Generation is the automated process of creating written content. It's a tricky task because making sure the generated text is coherent and semantically meaningful isn't easy.

Text generation finds use in various applications such as powering chatbots, generating automatic reports, and creating written content for websites. It also plays a significant role in more complex NLP tasks like machine translation and summarization.

6.1.2 Applications of NLP: NLP in Real-World Settings

NLP technologies find their applications in various real-world settings, ranging from everyday consumer applications to sophisticated business and research applications.

6.1.2.1 Search Engines

One of the most familiar uses of NLP is in search engines. When you type or speak a query, search engines use NLP to understand your intent and find relevant results. The 'autocomplete' suggestions provided by search engines is another NLP-powered feature that makes searching faster and more efficient.

6.1.2.2 Voice Assistants and Chatbots

Voice assistants like Siri, Alexa, and Google Assistant use NLP to understand

and respond to voice commands. They use NLP technologies such as speech recognition, text-to-speech, and natural language understanding to interact in a way that feels human.

Chatbots also lean heavily on NLP. They understand the customer's text or voice input (using Natural Language Understanding), have a dialogue with the customer (using Dialogue Management), and then generate a response that sounds human (using Natural Language Generation).

6.1.2.3 Information Extraction and Knowledge Graphs

NLP is key in pulling structured information from unstructured text data. This extracted information can be used to build Knowledge Graphs, which are networked databases filled with facts about the world. Search engines like Google use Knowledge Graphs to enhance search results with factual and contextually relevant information.

In a nutshell, Natural Language Processing (NLP) plays a critical role in many areas of Artificial Intelligence. By helping computers to understand and generate human language, NLP has opened up a wide range of applications that were previously thought to be exclusively human tasks.

6.2 Computer Vision: Enabling Computers to See

Computer Vision is an exciting branch of Artificial Intelligence (AI) that focuses on teaching computers to understand and interpret visual data from the world around us. This field aims to replicate the way humans perceive visual information, allowing computers to analyze and make sense of images or videos in much the same way we do.

6.2.1 Understanding Visual Data: Key Tasks in Computer Vision

Computer vision is all about understanding visual data. It performs a range of tasks, each dedicated to extracting and understanding information from images or videos. Here are some of the central tasks:

6.2.1.1 Object Detection and Classification

Object detection involves identifying specific objects within an image or video. This task includes figuring out where the object is (localization) and what type of object it is (classification).

Typically, the output of object detection algorithms is a box outlining each detected object, along with a label indicating what the object is. This ability has been crucial in areas such as self-driving cars, where the vehicle needs to detect and categorize objects like pedestrians, other vehicles, and traffic signs.

6.2.1.2 Facial Recognition

Facial Recognition is the task of identifying or verifying a person's identity based on their facial features. It works by comparing facial features from a given image with faces stored in a database.

This technology is widely used in several areas, like security (to unlock smartphones), surveillance (to spot individuals of interest in CCTV footage), and social media (to tag friends in photos).

6.2.1.3 Image Segmentation

Image Segmentation involves dividing a digital image into multiple segments or regions, each corresponding to different objects or areas of interest. Unlike object detection, which typically outlines objects with a box, image segmentation classifies each pixel in the image.

This technique is useful in many areas, like medical imaging, where it can help identify tumors or other irregularities, or in self-driving cars, to better understand the driving environment.

6.2.1.4 Optical Character Recognition (OCR)

Optical Character Recognition (OCR) is a technology that turns different types of documents - scanned paper documents, PDF files, or images captured by a digital camera - into editable and searchable data. This is a challenging task due to the variety of fonts, sizes, and styles of text in real-world documents.

OCR technology has transformed document management in sectors like banking, insurance, and healthcare, by reducing manual data entry and enabling efficient search and processing of text data in images.

6.2.2 Applications of Computer Vision: Translating Vision into Real-World Benefits

Computer Vision has a broad range of applications across various industries, providing automated and enhanced visual processing capabilities.

6.2.2.1 Facial Recognition Technology in Smartphones

Facial recognition technology has quickly become a standard feature in smartphones, revolutionizing device security. By recognizing the user's face, smartphones provide a secure and easy way to unlock devices. Moreover, facial recognition improves the user experience by enabling personalized services.

6.2.2.2 Medical Imaging Analysis

In healthcare, computer vision techniques analyze medical images for diagnostic purposes. They're used to identify abnormalities like tumors in MRI scans, spot retinal diseases in eye scans, and even predict heart diseases from chest X-rays.

6.2.2.3 Autonomous Vehicles

One of the most exciting applications of computer vision is in self-driving cars. These vehicles use computer vision systems to continually process visual data to detect and categorize objects, understand traffic signs, and perceive driving lanes. This information is vital for the decision-making and control systems of the vehicle.

To summarize, computer vision is a fundamental part of AI, enabling machines to understand and interpret the visual world. By doing this, it unlocks a wealth of potential for practical applications that can enhance our lives in terms of convenience, safety, and efficiency.

6.3 Robotics: Building Intelligent Machines

Robotics is – little surprising – all about designing, building, and operating robots and has become a global industry worth more than 38bn USD in 2022. While robotics isn't strictly a part of AI, incorporating AI technologies greatly boosts the abilities of robots. AI lets robots carry out complex tasks on their own, learn from their experiences, and interact more effectively with their environment.

6.3.1 Intersection of Robotics and AI: Autonomous Intelligence

When you bring robotics and AI together, you get machines that can make sense of their surroundings, make decisions based on what they perceive, and carry out actions that seemed impossible just years ago. AI equips robots with a form of intelligence, powering their abilities beyond just simple, preprogrammed tasks.

6.3.1.1 Perception and Understanding

Robots, when integrated with AI techniques like machine learning and computer vision, can perceive their environment in a manner similar to humans. They can identify objects, understand visual scenarios, and even interpret sounds. This level of perception is crucial for robots to interact effectively with the world around them.

6.3.1.2 Decision-making and Action

AI also gives robots the ability to make decisions. This might involve planning the quickest route to a destination, figuring out the best way to pick up an object, or even deciding how to interact with a human coworker. Once a decision is made, robots can then carry out the action using their physical components, changing their environment in the process.

6.3.1.3 Learning and Adaptation

One of the most fascinating aspects of AI in robotics is the ability for robots to learn from experience. With machine learning algorithms, robots can get better at their tasks over time, adapt to new situations, and even come up with new solutions to problems.

6.3.2 Applications of Robotics: AI-powered Robots in Action

AI-powered robots are making their mark in numerous areas and are slowly but surely transforming various industries and even our homes.

6.3.2.1 Manufacturing

Robots have been used in manufacturing for tasks like assembly, packaging, and inspection for a long time. However, adding AI capabilities allows for even more flexibility and efficiency. Robots can now work alongside humans in "cobot" arrangements, adapt to changes in components, and even fine-tune their workflows based on real-time data.

6.3.2.2 Healthcare

In healthcare, AI-powered robots help with a range of tasks. Robotic surgery systems, like the da Vinci Surgical System, offer minimally invasive surgery options with extreme precision. Robots also assist in patient care, helping with tasks like lifting patients, distributing medication, and even offering social interaction for elderly or isolated individuals.

6.3.2.3 Domestic Robots

In our homes, robots like the Roomba vacuum cleaner have become everyday items, taking care of tedious tasks. Personal assistant robots, equipped with AI, can communicate with users naturally, recognize different individuals, and even learn to better assist their users over time.

Robotics, enhanced by AI, offers a broad array of applications that are constantly evolving and expanding. From manufacturing to healthcare and even home use, AI-based robots continue to become a more important part of our everyday lives.

6.4 Major Fields of AI - Epilogue

With the completion of this chapter, you have completed your extensive introduction into the major fields of AI, witnessing firsthand how AI concepts and techniques are employed in Natural Language Processing, Computer Vision, and Robotics. These areas demonstrate the extraordinary range of AI, from understanding and generating human language to seeing the world as we do, and even interacting with it physically. Keep in mind the immense possibilities these fields offer as we continue into the second section of our book – generative AI.

For all of you who want to dive deeper into the world of AI, be referred to chapter 14 "Tools for AI Development", to be found in the beginning of the appendix at the end of this book. While I initially wanted to cover this topic in the main section of the book, I decided to put it into the appendix as not to overcrowd the main book and keep it practice-oriented.

PART II: GENERATIVE AI – FUNDAMENTAL CONCEPTS AND TECHNOLOGIES

Welcome to Part II: Generative AI. In this section of the book, we are going to take a deep dive into the rapidly emerging field of generative AI. Having completed "Part I: Artificial Intelligence", you now have a solid understanding of what AI is and the basic mechanisms, concepts and technologies it uses. This is a necessary foundation in order to have a clear understanding of generative AI, its various types, its functioning and the tremendous potential it holds – which will be the primary focus of this section.

So, without further ado, let's start diving in. To begin with, in the following chapter, we are going to take a 10.000-feet-overview of generative AI – after looking at the bigger picture, we are going to dissect the respective parts and aspects in separate sub-chapters. The goal is for you to become a Generative AI expert that can not only immediately make benefit of the amazing generative AI solutions out there but will also be able to enlighten others to the tremendous potential and impact this technology holds. Let's get started.

CHAPTER 7: INTRODUCTION TO GENERATIVE AI – THE 10.000 FOOT OVERVIEW

With the basics of AI behind us, it is time we discuss what Generative AI is and how it works. We will first start with a 10.000-ft overview of the field before we take a closer look at each respective element to make sure you can get a deep and detailed understanding of this most interesting of all AI fields.

To begin with, let's answer the most essential question of all:

7.1 What is Generative AI?

Generative AI refers to a type of artificial intelligence that uses machine learning models to produce outputs, such as text, images, or music, that are new and unique. It essentially allows computers to generate creative content that appears as though it could have been made by a human.

The term "generative" comes from the idea that these AI systems generate new data or content, rather than simply analyzing or processing existing data. In a sense, generative AI is about teaching machines to become creators. For example, generative AI can write a poem, draw a picture, or compose a song based on a given prompt.

The working principle of Generative AI models involves learning the underlying patterns and structures from a given dataset and then using this understanding to produce novel instances of data. They essentially emulate the data distribution of the training set, enabling them to generate new data that shares similar characteristics.

Generative Models vs. Discriminative Models:

AI models generally fall into two broad categories: generative and discriminative. Discriminative models learn the boundaries between different classes in a dataset, making them ideal for classification tasks. They answer questions like, "Given this data point, to which class does it belong?"

Generative models, on the other hand, learn the distribution of individual classes in the dataset. They're concerned with questions like, "Given this class, what might a data point from it look like?" This characteristic enables them to generate new data that resembles the original dataset.

7.2 How Does Generative AI Work?

At the heart of generative AI are algorithms known as generative models. These are a type of machine learning model that learns the underlying patterns in data and uses this understanding to generate new data.

Training a generative model involves providing it with a dataset and allowing it to learn the patterns, structures, and variations within this data. For instance, if we're training a model to generate images of cats, we'd feed it a large dataset of cat images. Over time, the model learns to understand what makes a cat image (the patterns of shapes, colors, textures, etc.) and can then generate new images that possess those same characteristics.

There are several different types of generative models, including but not limited to:

7.2.1 Generative Adversarial Networks (GANs)

Generative Adversarial Networks, or GANs, are like the art forgers of the machine learning world. But instead of creating unauthorized copies, they generate original, and often astonishingly lifelike, new creations.

Imagine a friendly competition between two artists. The first artist, we'll call her the "Generator", begins by sketching an image from her imagination. The second artist, let's call him the "Discriminator", plays the critic. His task is to compare the Generator's sketch to authentic sketches drawn from real life. If he can't distinguish the Generator's sketch from the real ones, the Generator wins. If he can, the Discriminator wins, and the Generator must try again.

In a GAN, the artists are replaced with two neural networks: the Generator network, which generates new data instances, and the Discriminator network, which evaluates them for authenticity. The Generator network begins the process by creating a sample. This sample is given to the Discriminator network alongside real data samples. The Discriminator network then attempts to classify each sample as either real or fake.

The fascinating aspect of GANs is their competitive dynamic. The Generator network is continuously learning to produce more and more convincing fake data, while the Discriminator network is continuously getting better at figuring out which data is real and which is the Generator's creation. This contest continues until the Generator network is so good at its job that the Discriminator network can't tell the difference anymore. At this point, the Generator is producing very convincing synthetic data.

But how does this manifest in real applications? One of the most well-known examples of GANs in action is their ability to create lifelike images of faces. These are faces of people who don't exist but could easily pass as real in a photograph. How can this be achieved? By training the Generator network on a vast dataset of real human faces. The Generator network learns the subtle patterns, shapes, and colors that make a face look real, and then uses this knowledge to create new faces.

Another fascinating application of GANs is in the field of art. Given a training set of famous paintings, for example, a GAN can learn the distinctive styles of various artists and produce new paintings that feel remarkably similar. These AI-generated artworks can have the appearance of being created by human hands, showcasing the uncanny creativity of GANs.

So, while the world of Generative Adversarial Networks might initially seem like a sci-fi novel, it is a very real and rapidly advancing field. The artworks, the faces, even the music that these AI models are creating today could be the poster children for the AI-generated content of tomorrow. With GANs, we're not just observing the art; we're peering into the creative mind of the AI itself.

7.2.2 Variational Autoencoders (VAEs)

Think of Variational Autoencoders as expert code-breakers in the world of AI, studying complex information, breaking it down to its simplest form, and then reconstructing it. They aim to understand data so well that they can create convincing replicas of the original.

Let's go back to our art analogy. A master art forger doesn't merely copy a painting stroke for stroke. They study it, understanding the artist's techniques, the color palette, the balance of elements, and the distinctive details that make the painting unique. After this deep study, they can then create a new painting in the same style that is almost indistinguishable from the original artist's work.

VAEs work in a somewhat similar way. They comprise two main components: an Encoder and a Decoder. The Encoder's job is to break down the input data into a simpler representation. It does this by compressing the data into a 'latent' or hidden space that captures the essential characteristics of the input.

Imagine taking a bustling cityscape and reducing it to a few key features: the tall skyscrapers, the winding river, the grid of streets. That's what the Encoder does — it condenses the complex input data into a lower-dimensional space that captures its most critical aspects.

Then comes the Decoder. Its task is to take this simplified representation and rebuild the original data from it. Using our cityscape example, the Decoder would take those key features — the skyscrapers, the river, the streets — and from these, reconstruct a cityscape that closely resembles the original one.

But VAEs don't stop at reproducing the original; they can generate entirely new examples that share the same essential features. Given a new set of key features, the Decoder can construct a new cityscape that's different from any it has seen before but still convincingly realistic.

VAEs find use in a myriad of applications. In the gaming industry, for instance, they can be used to generate new levels or characters based on a set of examples, allowing for a virtually infinite variety of gameplay experiences.

In the realm of 3D modeling, VAEs can learn from a collection of 3D objects and then create new objects that fit within the same category. For example, after studying a dataset of chairs, a VAE could generate the design for a new chair that's unlike any existing model but still unmistakably a chair.

Even in scientific fields like drug discovery, VAEs are making their mark. They can study the molecular structures of effective drugs and generate new molecular structures that might form the basis for new medicines.

7.2.3 Transformer-Based Models

To understand Transformers in the context of Generative AI, let's think of a professional translator sitting in the United Nations. This translator listens to what a speaker is saying, understands the context, and then translates that speech into another language. In doing so, the translator must understand the language structure, semantics, and the nuances of both the source and target languages. This is, in essence, the kind of job a Transformer model does in the AI world.

Transformers, introduced in the paper "Attention is All You Need" by Vaswani et al. (2017), are a type of model architecture used in natural language processing tasks, such as translation, summarization, and text generation. They are specifically designed to handle sequential data for tasks where the order of the data is essential, like in sentences or time-series data.

A key feature of Transformers is their attention mechanism, which differentiates them from previous sequential models like Recurrent Neural Networks (RNNs) or Long Short-Term Memory Networks (LSTMs). This mechanism allows the model to focus on different parts of the input sequence when producing an output, mimicking how a human translator might pay attention to different words when translating a sentence.

Let's delve into how Transformers handle text-to-text tasks:

The Transformer architecture comprises two main components: an Encoder and a Decoder.

Encoder: The Encoder's job is to take the input text and convert it into a meaningful representation that captures the text's context and semantics. It does this by passing the text through multiple layers of self-attention and feed-forward neural networks. The self-attention mechanism allows the model to weigh the importance of each word in the context of the entire sequence, enabling it to understand the dependencies between words, even those far apart in the sentence.

Decoder: Once the Encoder has transformed the input text into a set of high-dimensional vectors (each representing the semantic and contextual information of the input), it is the Decoder's turn. The Decoder, (also consisting of layers of self-attention and feed-forward neural networks, along with an additional layer of encoder-decoder attention), uses the encoded input to generate the output sequence, word by word.

The encoder-decoder attention layer allows the Decoder to focus on different parts of the input sequence, much like how a human translator would refer back to different words in the original sentence while translating. The output of each step in the Decoder is a word in the generated text.

As the Transformer moves from one word to the next, it feeds its previous outputs back into itself, using this feedback to generate the next word and so on. This process continues until the model produces an end-of-sequence token, signaling the completion of the text generation task.

One of the most well-known uses of Transformers in Generative AI is OpenAI's GPT-4 model, a massive language model capable of generating impressively human-like text. Given a prompt (like the start of a poem or a news article), GPT-3 uses a Transformer Decoder to generate a continuation of the text that can be indistinguishable from something a human might write.

In summary, Transformers are a powerful tool in the Generative AI toolkit, particularly for text-to-text tasks. By paying "attention" to the context and semantics of input text, they can generate surprisingly sophisticated and nuanced output, bringing us closer than ever to machines that truly understand and generate human language.

7.2.4 Autoregressive Models

To visualize an autoregressive model in the context of Generative AI, imagine a writer drafting a story. As they write each sentence, they're continuously referring back to what they've written before, using that context to decide the next word, sentence, or paragraph. An autoregressive model functions in a similar manner: it generates new outputs, like sentences, one part at a time, using the previously generated parts as a reference for generating the next one.

Autoregressive models have been used in many areas of machine learning, but their application in text generation tasks, particularly through models like the Recurrent Neural Network (RNN), has made a substantial impact on the field.

PixelRNN, a specific type of autoregressive model, was initially designed to generate images pixel by pixel. However, the core principles behind it can be extended to text generation tasks. Here's how it works.

Sequence Dependency: At the heart of an autoregressive model is the assumption that the probability of a part of the sequence (like a word in a sentence) depends on the preceding parts. In other words, the context matters. Just like our writer, the model uses the words it has generated so far to decide

54

the next word.

Generating the Sequence: The model starts with an initial input (like a starting word or a sentence) and then begins generating the next parts of the sequence one step at a time. After each step, the model feeds the generated part back into itself as part of the input for the next step. This process continues until the model generates a predefined end token, or until the generated sequence reaches a certain length.

Handling Temporal Dependencies: Autoregressive models like RNNs are particularly good at handling temporal dependencies because they process the sequence step-by-step and carry forward a 'hidden state' from one step to the next. This hidden state acts as a sort of memory, allowing the model to incorporate information from early in the sequence when deciding the next part.

In the context of text-to-text tasks, an autoregressive model could be used, for instance, to generate a continuation of a given sentence. It starts with the input sentence (or a part of it) and then generates the next word based on the words it has seen so far. This process continues, with the model generating one word at a time until it forms a complete sentence or paragraph.

Consider an example where we want to generate a continuation of the sentence, "Once upon a time". The model might generate the next word as "in", using the context of the fairy tale-like beginning. Then, given "Once upon a time in", it might generate "a faraway kingdom". Each step depends on the words generated so far, creating a coherent, contextually appropriate continuation.

In conclusion, autoregressive models bring a crucial aspect of human-like understanding to the task of Generative AI: the ability to use context. By referring back to what they have generated so far and using that information to decide the next step, these models can create remarkably sophisticated and coherent outputs, be it in text, images, or any other type of sequential data.

7.3 Applications of Generative AI

Generative AI has become a powerful tool with a plethora of applications spanning various sectors. These applications showcase the capacity of generative AI to create, modify, and enhance digital content across different formats, as well as its potential to revolutionize sectors as diverse as healthcare and gaming.

- **Content Creation**: The ability of AI to generate diverse forms of textual content, including articles, stories, poetry, and sales copy, is being harnessed in numerous ways. For instance, news agencies are deploying generative AI models for automated news reporting, reducing turnaround times and allowing journalists to focus on more complex stories. Meanwhile, in the digital marketing domain, personalized content generation driven by AI aids in delivering targeted advertisements and improving customer engagement.

- **Art and Music**: In the realm of arts, generative models are unlocking new frontiers of creativity. They're being used to produce unique paintings, intricate design patterns, and even to compose original music. These AI-aided creations push the boundaries of artistic expression and introduce new avenues for artists to explore.

- **Image and Video Generation**: Generative AI demonstrates impressive capabilities when it comes to visual media. It can create realistic images and videos from scratch, or modify existing ones. While this technology has been controversially known for powering 'deepfake' videos, it also has legitimate and creative uses, such as in video game design and virtual reality, where it can create immersive and dynamic environments.

- **Data Augmentation**: Another valuable application of generative AI lies in its ability to create synthetic data. This is particularly useful in situations where real data is scarce, sensitive, or imbalanced. By generating additional data for testing and training purposes, generative AI can bolster the performance of machine learning models and mitigate the risk of overfitting.

- **Drug Discovery**: Generative models in the healthcare and pharmaceutical sectors are transforming the traditional drug discovery process. By creating new molecular structures for potential drugs, these models significantly expedite what was once a time-consuming and costly process. Consequently, generative AI is poised to play a critical role in addressing new diseases and enhancing global healthcare outcomes.

With these varied applications, it is clear that generative AI holds immense potential to reshape many aspects of our world, offering improvements in efficiency, creativity, and customization.

7.4 How are Generative AI Models Developed?

Before you can become a proficient user of generative AI solutions, it helps tremendously to understand the basics of how such models are being built and developed in the first place. It is a multi-step process that involves several crucial stages, each contributing to the model's ability to generate new data that closely resembles its inputs. This journey, from data collection to deployment, involves not only technical considerations but also strategic decision-making based on the specific requirements of the task at hand.

- **Data Collection:** Generative models learn to create new data that resembles their input data, so the first step is gathering this input data. This might involve collecting images, text, or any other type of data the model will be generating.

- **Data Preprocessing:** The collected data may need to be cleaned or transformed into a suitable format for the model.

- **Model Selection:** The next step is to choose the type of generative model that's most suitable for the task at hand. This might depend on the type and amount of data available, the complexity of the task, and the resources available for training the model.

- **Model Training:** This involves presenting the model with the input data so that it can learn the underlying patterns or structure. This process typically uses a type of algorithm known as gradient descent to gradually improve the model's ability to generate data similar to its inputs.

- **Evaluation and Fine-Tuning:** Once the model has been trained, it is important to evaluate its performance and adjust its parameters or architecture as necessary. This might involve using human judgment (for tasks like image or text generation) or quantitative metrics (for tasks where the quality of the generated data can be objectively measured).

- **Deployment:** Once the model is performing well, it can be used to generate new data. Depending on the application, this might involve integrating the model into a software application, providing it as a service over the internet, or using it to generate a fixed set of data for a specific purpose.

- In the next section, we will delve into more detail about the types of generative models and the process of developing them. We will also explore the exciting applications and ethical considerations of generative AI.

7.5 The Types of Generative AI

There is not "just one" type of generative AI, there are various types of generative AI. The most common way to distinguish these is by the type of content being input and output. This is how you end up with the following 7 most common types of generative AI:

- **Text-to-Text (T2T) Generative AI**: These models are used to generate text based on a text input. They are often used in applications like machine translation, text summarization, and chatbots. Examples of this include GPT-4, Google Bard, and other Transformer-based models. You enter a text-based prompt, e.g., into ChatGPT and it will give you a text-based output.

- **Text-to-Audio (T2A) Generative AI:** Here, written text is converted into spoken words, typically for applications like text-to-speech (TTS) systems and audiobook creation. Google's Tacotron and Amazon's Polly are examples of this type of generative AI.

- **Text-to-Image (T2I) Generative AI**: T2I tools generate an image based on a description provided in text. An example of this is DALL-E from OpenAI or MidJourney, which can create images from textual descriptions.

- **Text-to-Video (T2V) Generative AI**: Such models can generate videos based on text input. However, such tools are currently still in their infancy, as text-to-video is a more complex task, involving the generation of a sequence of images that change over time in a way that makes sense given the input.

- **Text-to-Music (T2M) Generative AI**: T2M models generate music based on a text-based prompt. This might involve generating a melody based on a description or a set of instructions, or even creating a musical composition based on the mood or theme of a piece of text. OpenAI's MuseNet is an example of a model that can generate music in a variety of styles.

- **Audio-to-Text (A2T) Generative AI**: Also known as automatic speech recognition (ASR) systems, these models convert spoken language into written text. While not generative in the traditional sense (as they transcribe rather than create), they're still a critical part of the AI landscape. A2T is used in a variety of applications, including transcription services, voice assistants like Amazon's Alexa or Apple's Siri, and real-time captioning services for the hearing impaired. Examples include Google's Speech-to-Text API and IBM's Watson Speech to Text service.

- **Text-to-Code (T2C) Generative AI**: This type of generative AI converts natural language text into programming code. T2C AI models are used for tasks such as code generation, code completion, and even bug detection. The best example of this type of AI is GitHub Copilot, an AI-powered code assistant. When you type a comment or a piece of code, GitHub Copilot suggests ways to complete your line or block of code.

This diversity illustrates the flexibility and potential of generative AI tools for creativity and automation.

It is important to note that while all these types of generative AI models are exciting, they are also challenging to develop and perfect, requiring large amounts of data, computational resources, and careful tuning of model parameters. Furthermore, the outputs they produce may still be imperfect or unexpected, yet impressive nonetheless. Despite the rapid progress in this field, there is still much we don't know about teaching machines to generate complex, creative content – but millions of developers around the world are working overtime to overcome these issues.

CHAPTER 8: THE TYPES OF GENERATIVE AI

This chapter represents the beginning of our deep dive into the various aspects of generative AI we looked at shortly in chapter 7. We start with a closer look at the different types of generative AI and how they work, laying the foundation for a better understanding and ability to use the generative AI tools you may already be employing or wanting to use in your personal and professional lives.

The different types of Generative AI can be broadly categorized based on the form of output they generate: text, audio, images, video, or even code such that 7 important types of generative AI should be understood and characterized – Text-to-Text, Text-to-Image, Text-to-Video, Audio-to-Text, Image-to-Image, Video-to-Video/Video-to-image and Text-to-Code.

8.1 Text-to-Text

The advent of Text-to-Text Generative AI models marks a significant milestone in AI's ability to mimic human-like text generation, making substantial impacts across various fields. You have most definitely come into contact with text-to-text generative AI if you have ever used ChatGPT, Bing Chat or Google Bard.

8.1.1 Detailed Understanding of Text-to-Text Generative AI Functionality

Text-to-Text AI models operate through a meticulous process of training and learning from an extensive range of written language datasets. They can comprehend the intricacies of human language, including syntax, semantics, and cultural nuances.

8.1.1.1 Training Phase

During the training phase, these models consume an enormous corpus of text data, such as billions of websites scraped from the internet (like OpenAI did with GPT-3 and GPT-4), learning the underlying patterns and statistical structures that govern the use of language. For instance, a model might learn the grammatical rules of English, the general structure of sentences, or common phrases used in specific contexts. The process is not programmed explicitly; instead, the models 'infer' these rules by analyzing the statistical relationships between words, phrases, and sentences in the data.

8.1.1.2 Generation Phase

Once they have been trained, T2T models can generate text by taking a piece of input text (or prompt) and predicting what comes next based on what it has learned. The output retains the statistical properties of the input data, which is why the resulting text appears coherent and relevant to the context the input provided.

8.1.2 Expanding on the Applications

Text-to-Text Generative AI models find extensive use in numerous fields, thanks to their ability to produce text that mirrors human writing. The applications range from automating content creation to facilitating language translation.

Automated Content Creation

In the realm of content creation, these models are equipped to draft articles, reports, and creative pieces with a high level of coherence and relevance. The AI can produce content on various topics, given it has been trained on a diverse and comprehensive dataset. Businesses, content marketers, and journalists find this especially useful, as it augments their capacity to generate content swiftly and efficiently.

Chatbots and Virtual Assistants

Chatbots and virtual assistants are perhaps the most common application of Text-to-Text AI models. These AI-powered tools are now capable of producing human-like responses in a conversation, making them sound less robotic and more natural. By generating responses that are contextually appropriate, these models can lead intelligent conversations, enhancing user experience.

Language Translation

Language translation is another crucial application of Text-to-Text AI. These models can learn multiple languages and their nuances, allowing them to translate text from one language to another while retaining the original context and meaning. This application extends to real-time translation services, making cross-cultural communication more accessible and efficient.

By delving deeper into Text-to-Text Generative AI, we gain a broader understanding of its potential to revolutionize various fields, from content creation to customer service and beyond.

8.1.3 OpenAI's GPT Series: Perfection of Text-to-Text

The GPT series by OpenAI, including GPT-3 and GPT-4, serves as the prime examples of Text-to-Text Generative AI models. These models generate human-like text, which is contextually relevant, and can mimic human traits such as creativity and humor. With such a level of sophistication, these tools may be employed in a variety of applications, from writing articles and generating code to creating poetry and even cracking jokes.

> In conclusion, Text-to-Text Generative AI models serve as a critical tool in numerous applications, propelling advancements in fields like customer service, content creation, and language services. As these models continue to improve and evolve, they hold the potential to reshape our interaction with text-based digital interfaces.

8.1.4 Case Study 1: Magazine Implements Text-to-Text AI to Scale Article Generation

In the following, we have an anonymized case study by an online magazine that has implemented the generative AI tools ChatGPT and Jasper to transform their content creation process. The anonymization has been necessary, as the respective project managers wouldn't allow me to share more details of their company.

Magazine Y: How ChatGPT and Jasper Transformed Their Content Creation Process

Magazine Y is a weekly publication that covers topics such as health, wellness, fitness, and nutrition. The magazine has a team of 10 writers and editors who produce around 50 articles per week for the print and online editions.

The magazine faced several challenges in creating high-quality and engaging content for its readers. Some of these challenges were:

- Generating fresh and original ideas for new articles
- Writing catchy headlines and introductions that capture the readers' attention
- Creating relevant and informative content that matches the readers' interests and needs
- Adding visual elements such as images and graphs to enhance the content
- Editing and proofreading the articles for grammar, spelling, and style errors
- Meeting the tight deadlines and publishing schedules

To overcome these challenges, Magazine Y decided to use text-to-text AI tools to assist its writers and editors in their content creation process. The magazine used the following tools:

- ChatGPT: With ChatGPT, the magazine generated fresh and original ideas for new articles by entering a general topic or category as a prompt. ChatGPT would then generate a list of possible subtopics or angles that the writers could explore or write about. The magazine also used ChatGPT to generate catchy headlines and introductions for each article by entering the main topic or idea as a prompt. ChatGPT would then generate several variations of headlines and introductions that the writers could choose from or modify as needed.

- Jasper: An AI art generator & writer that can create amazing content faster. The magazine used Jasper to create relevant and informative content that matches the readers' interests and needs by entering a few keywords or sentences as a prompt. Jasper would then generate a long-form text that covers the topic in depth and provides useful tips and advice. The magazine also used Jasper to add visual elements such as images and graphs to enhance the content by entering a text description as a prompt. Jasper would then generate an image or a graph that matches the description and complements the content.

By using these text-to-text AI tools, Magazine Y was able to transform its content creation process significantly. Some of the benefits that the magazine experienced were:

- Saving time and effort in generating fresh and original ideas for new articles

- Increasing the click-through rate and engagement of the readers with catchy headlines and introductions

- Enhancing the relevance and informativeness of the content with AI-generated texts

- Improving the visual appeal of the content with AI-generated images and graphs

- Reducing the errors and mistakes in the content with automated editing and proofreading

- Meeting the deadlines and publishing schedules with faster and easier content creation

All in all, Magazine Y was very satisfied with the results of using text-to-text AI tools and plans to continue using them in the future. While it is too early to clearly calculate how much time and money these tools have saved them, the project manager estimates the time savings to be between 40-55 % and cost savings up to 70 %. He also stated that they intend to explore other T2T AI tools that can help with other aspects of content creation, such as generating summaries, captions, or translations.

8.1.5 Case Study 2: Copywriter Scales Copywriting Business with Text-to-

Text AI Solutions

Copywriter Z is a freelance copywriter who specializes in writing sales pages, landing pages, email sequences, and social media posts for online businesses. He has been working as a copywriter for over five years and has built a loyal client base and a strong portfolio. Through our excessive debates and communication on Reddit and Discord, I was able to get him to write a case study for the sake of this book.

Copywriter Z faced several challenges in growing his copywriting business and delivering high-quality and engaging copy for his clients. Some of these challenges were:

- Generating fresh and original ideas for each copywriting project
- Writing catchy headlines and hooks that capture the readers' attention
- Creating persuasive and compelling copy that converts
- Adding visual elements such as images and emojis to enhance the copy
- Editing and proofreading the copy for grammar, spelling, and style errors
- Meeting the tight deadlines and client expectations

To overcome these challenges, Copywriter Z decided to use text-to-text AI tools to assist him in his copywriting process. He used both ChatGPT and Jasper. While all of our readers are probably somewhat familiar with ChatGPT, few might have heard about Jasper which is an AI art generator & writer that can create amazing content faster. Copywriter Z used Jasper to create persuasive and compelling copy that converts by entering a few keywords or sentences as a prompt. Jasper would then generate a long-form text that covers the topic in depth and provides benefits, features, testimonials, guarantees, and more. Personally, Z prefers to use ChatGPT for the creation of a list of possible angles, headlines, hooks, bullet points, calls to action, and more that he could use or modify as needed.

Overall, using ChatGPT and Jasper, Copywriter Z has achieved a tremendous growth and optimization of his copywriting processes. The most essential benefits he has achieved are:

- Saving time and effort in generating fresh and original ideas for each copywriting project
- Increasing the click-through rate and conversion rate of his clients with catchy headlines and hooks
- Enhancing the persuasiveness and compellingness of his copy with AI-generated texts
- Improved visual appeal of his copy with AI-generated images and emojis
- Fewer errors and mistakes in his copy with automated editing and

proofreading
- Meeting the deadlines and client expectations with faster and easier copywriting

Copywriter Z was very satisfied with the results of using text-to-text AI tools and decided to scale up his copywriting business. He hired two more writers to join him and trained them on how to use ChatGPT and Jasper effectively. He also increased his rates and expanded his services to include more types of copywriting projects. He now runs a successful copywriting agency that uses text-to-text AI tools as an integral part of its workflow.

8.2 Text-to-Image

Text-to-Image AI models are a fascinating blend of natural language processing (NLP) and computer vision technologies. They are capable of taking a text prompt as input and producing a relevant image as output, thereby converting semantic descriptions into corresponding visual symbols.

8.2.1 Training Phase

In the training phase, Text-to-Image AI models are exposed to a large dataset containing images paired with corresponding textual descriptions. This process enables them to understand the relationship between specific phrases in the text and elements in the images. For instance, the phrase "blue sky" would be associated with an image portion representing a blue-colored sky.

8.2.2 Generation Phase

During the generation phase, the models use the learned text-image relationship to generate images from new text inputs. When provided with a text prompt, the model discerns the semantic meaning and constructs a corresponding image by arranging visual symbols, colors, and shapes that it has learned to associate with specific text phrases.

8.2.3 Expanding on the Applications

Text-to-Image Generative AI models are most commonly used in areas demanding a visual representation of ideas, ranging from art and design to scientific visualization. Especially graphic designers have learned to love and fear them, profiting from enormous time savings but sometimes fearing for their professional future given the enormous speed in the improvement of these models.

Art and Design

In the realm of art and design, these AI models can be instrumental in catalyzing the creative process. Artists and designers can provide a text description of their envisioned artwork or design, and the AI can generate a visual draft based on that description. This application can speed up the initial design phase and help visual artists translate their ideas into tangible forms more quickly.

Scientific Visualization

Another substantial application lies in the scientific domain, where complex concepts often require clear visual representation for better understanding. Text-to-Image AI models can generate diagrams or illustrations based on scientific descriptions, providing a valuable tool for science educators and researchers. These models can convert textual descriptions of scientific phenomena into visual diagrams, thereby making complex concepts more accessible and engaging.

As we delve deeper into Text-to-Image Generative AI, we uncover the remarkable potential of these models in enhancing our ability to visualize ideas and concepts across various disciplines.

8.2.4 Case Study 1: How Graphic Designer W used TTI Tools to Scale His Design Business and Hire Two More Designers

Graphic Designer W is a freelance graphic designer who specializes in creating logos, flyers, posters, and social media graphics for small businesses and entrepreneurs. He has been working as a graphic designer for over three years and has built a loyal client base and a strong portfolio.

W always intended to grow his business, but he was faced with significant challenges and constraints in his prior work. Some of these challenges were:

- Generating fresh and original ideas for each design project
- Creating visually appealing and professional graphics that match the clients' brand identity and message
- Adding relevant and informative content such as text, icons, and charts to enhance the graphic.
- Editing and modifying the graphics according to the clients' feedback and preferences
- Meeting the tight deadlines and client expectation.

To overcome these challenges, W decided to use text-to-image AI tools to assist him in his design process. He used the following tools:

- Adobe Firefly
- MidJourney

Using these TTI tools, W was able to scale his design business significantly. Some of the benefits that he experienced were:

- Saving time and effort in generating fresh and original ideas for each design project
- Increasing the satisfaction and loyalty of his clients with visually appealing and professional graphics

- Enhancing the relevance and informativeness of his graphics with AI-generated texts
- Improving the visual appeal of his graphics with AI-generated images and emojis
- Reducing the errors and mistakes in his graphics with automated editing and modifying
- Meeting the deadlines and client expectations with faster and easier design

W continues to be very satisfied with the results and productivity gains he has gotten from becoming an expert on TTI tools and generative AI. In fact, he has become so successful, that he was finally able to scale up his design business. He hired two more designers to join him and trained them on how to use Adobe Firefly and MidJourney effectively. He also increased his rates and expanded his services to include more types of design projects. He now runs a successful design agency that uses text-to-image AI tools as an integral part of its workflow.

8.2.5 Case Study 2: How Gaming Company U Used Text-to-Image AI Tools To Streamline Their Internal Operations and Boost Productivity

Gaming Company V is a small indie game studio that develops and publishes casual games for mobile platforms. The company has a team of 15 developers, designers, artists, and testers who work on various aspects of game development. I was particularly thrilled to have a 1-hour Zoom call with their product manager to discuss how text-to-image AI has completely transformed their sketching and design work.

The company faced several challenges in creating high-quality and engaging games for its target audience. Some of these challenges were:

- Coming up with fresh and original design ideas for new games
- Creating realistic and appealing graphics for the game characters, environments, and objects
- Adding relevant and informative content such as text, icons, and sounds to enhance the game experience
- Editing and modifying the graphics according to the game design and feedback
- Meeting the tight deadlines and budget constraints (the gaming industry is among the most competitive in the world)

To overcome these challenges, U decided to use text-to-image AI tools to assist them in their game development process. They used the following tools:

- DALL-E 2
- Adobe Firefly

By using these tools, U was able to streamline their internal operations and boost their productivity significantly. Some of the benefits that they experienced were:

- Saving time and effort in generating fresh and original ideas for new games
- Increasing the satisfaction and loyalty of their players with realistic and appealing graphics
- Enhancing the relevance and informativeness of their games with AI-generated texts
- Improving the visual appeal of their games with AI-generated images and emojis
- Reducing the errors and mistakes in their games with automated editing and modifying
- Meeting the deadlines and budget constraints with faster and easier game development

The gaming company was thrilled by the productivity gains and cost and time savings they were able to realize within the first two months of starting to work with AI. Their efficiency gains provided the budget necessary to hire three more developers and designers to join them and speed up time-to-market for new games significantly. They also increased their revenue and expanded their portfolio to include more types of games.

8.3 Text to Video

Text-to-Video Generative AI models are an exciting advancement in the field of generative AI. They offer the ability to interpret text-based descriptions and generate a corresponding video, crafting a sequence of moving images that accurately represent the textual input.

8.3.1 Detailed Understanding of Text-to-Video Generative AI Functionality

The underlying functionality of Text-to-Video AI is basically a powerful fusion of Text-to-Image and Video Generative AI capabilities. These models are designed to interpret the semantic content of the input text, generate relevant static images, and ensure a logical and temporal coherence between the images to create a smooth, flowing video.

Training Phase

During the training phase, Text-to-Video models are exposed to extensive datasets of videos along with their corresponding textual descriptions. This exposure helps the model learn how textual prompts relate to the sequential visual scenes in the videos.

Generation Phase

In the generation phase, when provided with a new text input, the model interprets the semantics of the text and generates a series of relevant images. The model then sequences these images while maintaining temporal coherence, effectively creating a video that aligns with the input text.

8.3.2 Expanding on the Applications

Text-to-Video Generative AI models present several valuable applications, particularly in the fields of film and animation, education, and training.

Film and Animation

The film and animation industry stands to profit immensely from these AI models, particularly in assisting the storyboard creation process. The models can generate visual drafts or even rudimentary animations from script descriptions, providing film and animation creators with a visual representation of their scripts and saving considerable time in the initial stages of production.

Education and Training

In educational settings, Text-to-Video AI models can generate illustrative videos based on educational content, such as textbook paragraphs or lecture notes. The ability to convert text-based educational content into video form can greatly enhance students' understanding and engagement by catering to visual learning preferences.

Indeed, TTV AI offers enormous potential in various domains, particularly those that can benefit from transforming textual content into dynamic, visual experiences.

8.4 Audio-to-Text

Audio-to-Text AI or Speech-to-Text (STT) performs the function of transcribing spoken language into written text. This technology is at the heart of services like automated transcription, voice commands, and real-time captioning, broadening accessibility and enhancing convenience in various applications.

Given their capability to translate spoken language into written text, STT is an incredibly versatile AI technology that is increasingly used across multiple sectors and domains.

8.4.1 Unpacking the Functionality of Audio-to-Text Generative AI

To fully appreciate the capabilities of Audio-to-Text Generative AI, we must look beyond the surface and investigate the intricate process that enables these models to perform such a complex task.

Audio Signal Analysis

The initial phase in the Audio-to-Text conversion involves the analysis of the audio signal. The STT model receives the audio input and starts the process of deciphering it. Here, the spoken language is broken down into the smallest discernible units of sound, known as phonemes.

Language Modeling and Transcription

Following the audio signal analysis, the model applies language modeling to the identified phonemes. This process is based on vast databases of linguistic data, which help the model recognize words and sentence structures. Through this, the AI model can accurately transcribe the phonemes into written text, preserving the meaning and context of the original spoken language.

8.4.2 Exploring Applications of Audio-to-Text Generative AI

Audio-to-Text Generative AI has a broad range of applications across various industries and sectors – let us look at them in more detail below:

Transcription Services

Automated transcription of audio files into written text is one of the primary uses of STT models. This service is highly sought after in several sectors, such as law, healthcare, and media. Lawyers may need audio recordings transcribed for case files, doctors want to have their dictated notes transcribed, and media organizations often transcribe interviews and speeches.

Voice-Controlled Systems

STT technology is the backbone of voice-controlled and voice-responsive systems. These include virtual assistants like Amazon's Alexa or Apple's Siri, and other smart devices that respond to voice commands. By accurately transcribing spoken instructions into text, these devices can interpret and execute a wide range of commands.

Understanding the inner workings and applications of Audio-to-Text Generative AI allows us to recognize its transformative potential and foresee the new possibilities it is yet to unlock.

Enhancing Accessibility: Real-Time Captioning

The real-time conversion of speech into text has significant implications for accessibility. Real-time captioning, also known as live captioning or automatic captioning, is extensively used in broadcasting, online video platforms, and live events to ensure accessibility for the deaf and hard of hearing community.

In conclusion, the transformative potential of Audio-to-Text Generative AI is well-recognized, with its applications offering solutions to accessibility barriers, hands-free device interactions, and efficient transcription services. The continued advancement in this technology holds promising prospects for the future.

8.5 Image-to-Image

Known as "I2I" or Image-to-Image AI models, this type of generative AI involves transformative models that accept an image as input and generate a different, often enhanced or stylized, image as output. These AI models exemplify the expanding capabilities of Generative AI beyond text and audio generation.

8.5.1 Technical Underpinnings of Image-to-Image AI

I2I generative AI operates on the principles of advanced machine learning, pattern recognition, and deep learning. These models leverage neural networks with many layers (deep networks) that are adept at understanding the complex features and attributes of the input images. Consequently, they generate output images that retain key characteristics of the input while introducing unique modifications.

8.5.2 Notable Applications of Image-to-Image AI

- **Image Colorization:** These models can add color to black and white images, effectively transforming them into colored versions while maintaining their authenticity. This has applications in restoring old photographs and films, or even in interpreting historical images in a new light.

- **Super-resolution:** Image-to-Image AI can enhance the quality of low-resolution images, a process known as super-resolution. By inferring missing details, they generate high-resolution versions of input images, which is particularly useful in surveillance, medical imaging, and digital forensics.

- **Style Transfer:** Style transfer is a fascinating application where the artistic style of one image is applied to another. With this ability, users can transform regular images into artwork mirroring the styles of famous painters, for example.

8.5.3 Emphasizing GANs: The Powerhouse of Image Generation

Generative Adversarial Networks (GANs) are a pivotal form of Image-to-Image Generative AI. Introduced by Ian Goodfellow and his colleagues in 2014, GANs consist of two neural networks — the generator and the discriminator — competing in a zero-sum game. The generator aims to create realistic images, while the discriminator's goal is to distinguish these generated images from real ones.

The adversarial relationship between these two networks results in the generator improving its output until the discriminator can no longer tell the difference between real and generated images. GANs have been used to generate astonishingly realistic images, from faces of non-existent people to high-definition landscape images, and have immense potential in fields like entertainment, design, and virtual reality.

8.6 Video-to-Video and Video-to-Image Generative AI

Video Generative AI is an extension of image generative models to videos or moving images, necessitating the model to understand and generate data in four dimensions - height, width, color channels, and now, time. This additional complexity makes these models more challenging to develop but also presents even more versatile applications.

8.6.1 Core Mechanisms and Challenges of Video Generative AI

The principle behind Video Generative AI involves understanding the temporal correlations within a sequence of frames that constitute a video. Much like an Image-to-Image Generative AI learns the distribution of patterns in a static image, Video Generative AI must grasp the distribution of patterns across dynamic frames. This includes not just spatial patterns within each frame, but also the way these patterns evolve over time.

Handling the time dimension does, however, present additional challenges. The volume of data in videos is significantly larger, as videos are essentially sequences of images. This increases the computational complexity. Moreover, it is critical to maintain the temporal coherence (ensuring successive frames are logically connected in time), adding an additional layer of complexity.

8.6.2 Diverse Applications of Video Generative AI

- **Video Synthesis:** Much like Image-to-Image synthesis, Video Generative AI can generate one video from another, like turning a day scene into night or altering the weather in a video.

- **Video Prediction:** These models can predict future frames of a video based on the previous frames. This can be useful in numerous areas, from predicting the movement of vehicles or pedestrians for autonomous driving systems, to forecasting natural phenomena for environmental monitoring.

- **Generating Videos from Textual Descriptions:** There is ongoing research into models that can generate videos directly from textual descriptions. Imagine feeding a text such as "A dog is playing with a ball in a park" to an AI, and it produces a video clip that fits the description.

- **Video-to-Image Generation:** Some models are designed to extract representative images or summaries from a video, which can aid in video compression, editing, and content management.

While Video Generative AI is complex and computationally challenging, it holds promise for significant advancements in fields ranging from entertainment and media to surveillance and autonomous driving systems. With continued research and development, these models will undoubtedly continue to improve, opening up even more potential applications.

8.7 Text-to-Code

Text-to-code generative AI describes AI systems that use NLP to understand text-based prompts and then generate corresponding programming code – reaching from single snippets of code to entire applications or smart contracts.

The basic working of a text-to-code generative AI is similar to any other language translation task performed by AI. It takes an input in one language (in this case, natural language text) and translates it into another language (in this case, programming code).

8.7.1 How it works

- **Training:** The AI is trained on a large dataset of examples where natural language instructions and corresponding programming code are paired together. The AI learns the mappings from text instructions to code snippets by processing this data.

- **Generation:** Once trained, given a new text instruction, the AI predicts the corresponding code. It does this by breaking down the instruction into parts and generating code for each part, which it then assembles into a complete code snippet.

8.7.2 Features of text-to-code generative AI:

- **Multi-language support:** It can support multiple programming languages, such as Python, Java, C#, etc. For example, OpenAI Codex is the model based on GPT-3 that powers GitHub Copilot, a tool that can write code in at least a dozen languages.

- **Contextual understanding:** It can handle various types of tasks, such as web development, data analysis, game design, etc. For example, CodeT5 is an open source programming language model that can generate code based on natural language descriptions.

- **Error correction:** It can provide feedback and suggestions to improve the quality and efficiency of the code. For example, Tabnine is an AI-based code completion tool that can suggest relevant code snippets and correct errors.

- **Self-learning:** It can learn from existing code repositories and online resources to enhance its knowledge and skills. For example, OpenAI Codex is trained on billions of lines of code available in the public domain, such as GitHub repositories.

8.7.3 Notable applications of text-to-code generative AI

- **Rapid Prototyping:** Developers can use it to quickly prototype software by giving high-level instructions instead of writing every single line of code.

- **Non-technical Users:** People without coding experience can use it to create simple scripts or automate tasks.

- **Educational Purposes**: It can be used to assist in learning programming languages by providing code examples for given instructions.

- **Accessibility**: It can make programming more accessible to people who struggle with traditional coding due to disabilities.

> Text-to-code generative AI is a fascinating and promising technology that could revolutionize the field of software development and beyond. Already, tools like ChatGPT and GitHub Copilot show that the ever-persistent shortage of developers around the world could soon be upended by generative AI.

8.8 Image-to-Video

The name already gives it away: with this type of generative AI tool, you can take images like photos or graphics as inputs and turn them into shorter or longer video sequences.

It can use a single image or a series of images as input, and generate a video output that matches the content, style, and format of the input. The core technology to this capability are deep learning models that help the AI to understand the input and synthesize realistic and relevant graphics.

8.8.1 How it works

Image-to-video generative AI works by using two main components: an encoder and a decoder. The encoder is a neural network that takes the input image or images and extracts their features, such as the objects, colors, shapes, and textures. The decoder is another neural network that takes the features and generates a video output that preserves or transforms them. The decoder can also use additional information, such as text prompts, audio files, or video clips, to guide the generation process.

It is important to consider that encoder and decoder are trained together using large datasets of images and videos, so that they can learn how to produce high-quality and consistent outputs.

8.8.2 Features of image-to-video generative AI

Some of the features of image to video generative AI are:

- **Image input**: Such tools can create videos from various types of images, such as photos, drawings, sketches, or paintings.

- **Style customization**: It can generate videos with different styles, colors, fonts, and layouts, depending on the input or the user's preferences.

- **Video settings**: It can generate videos with different durations, speeds, and resolutions, depending on the input or the user's preferences.

- **Effect options**: It can generate videos with different effects, such as motion, animation, water, clouds, fire, or smoke, depending on the input or the user's preferences.

- **Text format**: It can generate videos with text in a specific format in the image, such as speech bubbles, captions, or sound effects.

8.8.3 Notable applications of image-to-video generative AI

Image to video generative AI solutions are particularly useful for the following scenarios and use cases:

- **Rapid Prototyping:** Designing slideshows, presentations, ads, or social media posts from photos or drawings.

- **Non-technical Users**: Making fun or creative content, such as memes, comics, or cartoons from sketches or images.

- **Educational Purposes**: Enhancing or editing existing videos with new graphics or effects from images or text prompts.

- **Accessibility**: Experimenting with different generative AI tools and models for image generation.

CHAPTER 9: BENEFITS OF DOWNSIDES OF GENERATIVE AI

In this chapter, we examine the double-edged sword of Generative AI. We discuss the vast possibilities it opens up, from content creation, data augmentation, and anomaly detection to its role in driving innovation and increasing accessibility. However, we also grapple with the ethical dilemmas and challenges it presents, such as control over its outputs, disinformation potential, privacy concerns, and inherent bias. Let's go.

9.1 Benefits of Generative AI

- **Content Creation:** One of the most compelling uses of generative AI is its ability to create new content, including images, text, music, and more. This automated content generation can be used across numerous fields. For instance, in entertainment, generative AI models can create original pieces of music or help script television shows. In advertising, AI can generate catchy taglines or design promotional images. Journalists can use these models to draft articles, especially for data-heavy reports like sports or financial news. Even in scientific research, AI helps to draft research papers or create illustrative diagrams.

- **Data Augmentation:** Generative AI has proven extremely useful in creating synthetic data that can augment existing datasets. This is particularly beneficial when dealing with limited or imbalanced data, which is a common issue in machine learning. By generating new data samples, generative AI can help improve the performance of machine learning models by reducing overfitting and bias and thereby making the models more accurate and reliable.

- **Cost-Effective:** Since it automates tasks that traditionally require human creativity or input, generative AI can save significant time and resources. Whether it is creating digital art for a marketing campaign, composing background music for a video, or writing reports, generative AI models can accomplish these tasks quickly and efficiently, freeing up human time for more complex and strategic activities.

- **Personalization:** Generative AI systems might leverage user data to create personalized content that caters to individual preferences and behaviors. This capability is particularly valuable in sectors like e-commerce, where personalized product recommendations can boost sales, or in digital entertainment, where customized content can enhance user engagement. In education, personalized learning materials generated by AI can improve learning outcomes.

- **Prototyping:** In industries like architecture, product design, or video game development, generative AI can be employed to create prototypes or simulations. AI can quickly generate multiple design variations, allowing designers to explore a broader range of options and choose the best one. This can significantly speed up the design process and lead to more innovative outcomes.

- **Anomaly Detection:** Generative AI models learn the normal distribution or patterns of data, which can be used to identify outliers or anomalies. This is crucial in fields like cybersecurity, where unusual network activity may indicate a cyber attack, or in healthcare, where anomalous medical images may signal a disease. By identifying anomalies, generative AI can help prevent potential issues before they escalate.

- **Increased Accessibility:** Generative AI can make information more accessible by transforming one type of content into another. For example, text-to-speech AI models can help visually impaired individuals access written content, and speech-to-text models can assist hearing-impaired individuals in understanding spoken language. Thus, generative AI plays a vital role in creating inclusive digital environments.

- **Predictive Capabilities:** Working with time-series data, generative AI models can predict future data points based on the patterns learned from historical data. For use cases in the finance industry, this could mean predicting stock prices or market trends. In healthcare, it might involve forecasting disease outbreaks or patient outcomes. For weather forecasts, generative AI helps to predict the likelihood of possible future weather patterns. These predictive capabilities can help make proactive decisions and strategies.

- **Innovation:** By generating new and unexpected combinations of ideas, generative AI offers a powerful tool for creativity and innovation. It can serve as a source of inspiration, offering solutions or ideas that might not be intuitive to humans. Whether it is creating a unique piece of artwork, devising a novel product design, or coming up with an innovative strategy, generative AI can push the boundaries of what's possible.

- **Privacy Preservation:** Generative AI can generate synthetic datasets that maintain the statistical properties of the original data but do not contain any personally identifiable information. This is crucial in an era where privacy concerns are growing by the day. By creating and working with synthetic data, researchers and organizations can perform data analysis and model training without violating privacy regulations or ethical norms.

9.2 Downsides of Generative AI

While Generative AI has immense potential, it also presents significant challenges and ethical considerations. Hence, in this section, we are going to address these aspects and concerns.

- **Content Manipulation**: While generative AI's capacity to create new content is promising, it also introduces the risk of content manipulation. For instance, 'deepfake' technology can create realistic yet falsified images, videos or audio recordings, potentially leading to misinformation, identity theft, or fraud. Additionally, AI-generated content may lack the creative nuances and emotional depth that human creators bring to their work.

- **Data Dependence**: Generative AI models heavily rely on the quality and quantity of data they are trained on. If the input data is biased or flawed, the output will reflect the same, leading to skewed results. This can be particularly damaging in sensitive areas like law enforcement or credit scoring, where biased AI models could reinforce societal biases.

- **High Costs**: Although generative AI can be cost-effective, the initial setup and maintenance costs can be high. Training large-scale generative AI models requires significant computational resources and energy, making it expensive. Smaller companies or startups might find it difficult to afford these costs.

- **Privacy Concerns**: Generative AI is able to generate synthetic data that preserves privacy, yet it might also infringe on privacy when it uses real user data for personalization purposes. There are potential risks of data misuse or breach, which could compromise personal information.

- **Over-Reliance on AI**: Exactly because of its efficiency and high-quality outputs, companies might start to overly rely on generative AI systems, potentially leading to a lack of human oversight. The need for human intervention and judgement remains important, especially when dealing with complex, nuanced tasks that require human empathy and understanding.

- **Job Displacement**: As generative AI takes over tasks traditionally performed by humans, there's a risk of job displacement. While AI can create new job opportunities, it can also render certain roles obsolete, leading to employment concerns.

- **Misaligned Expectations**: Generative AI models might not always meet user expectations. The gap between what users want and what the AI generates can lead to dissatisfaction. This is particularly the case with more creative outputs, like music or art, where human taste can be highly subjective and nuanced.

- **Exploitation**: There is a risk of generative AI being used maliciously, such as for generating spam or phishing emails, automating cyber attacks, or producing inappropriate or harmful content. The widespread availability of these tools can make them accessible to malicious actors.

- **Difficulty in Attribution**: With generative AI, it's challenging to attribute created content to a particular individual or entity. This can raise questions around copyright and ownership. Who owns AI-generated art or music, for instance?

- **Lack of Transparency**: Generative AI models, especially those based on deep learning, are often seen as 'black boxes'. It's hard to understand how they make their decisions, which can make them unpredictable and difficult to trust. This lack of transparency can be problematic in fields where accountability and interpretability are crucial, like healthcare or the legal sector.

Just like any technology, the use of generative AI comes with its own set of challenges and drawbacks. It's important to have regulations and guidelines in place to manage these potential issues and ensure that the technology is used responsibly and ethically.

PART III: PRACTICAL APPLICATIONS AND FUTURE DIRECTIONS

CHAPTER 10: THE TOP 7 GENERATIVE AI SOLUTIONS FOR END CONSUMERS AND HOW TO USE THEM

Now that we have looked at the fundamental concepts and technology behind Generative AI, it is time to look at the fun part – the practical application. Most likely this is the real reason you decided to invest into this book in the first place!

In this chapter, we will introduce you to the top 10 Generative AI solutions currently available to end consumers. From ChatGPT to GenCraft, we'll explore each tool's capabilities and offer guidance on how to use them effectively. From text-to-text, stunning text-to-image capabilities to the promised future of text-to-video, it is all here!

10.1 ChatGPT (by OpenAI)

Certainly you have heard of ChatGPT, the sensational AI chatbot that interacts with users in a natural and engaging way. It can answer questions, generate content, tell jokes, and have conversations on various topics and much much more. And since ChatGPT Plugins were rolled out to Plus users in May 2023, it has gotten dozens of new amazing capabilities.

The History of ChatGPT

The world's leading AI chatbot was developed by OpenAI, a research organization dedicated to creating and ensuring the safe and beneficial use of AI. ChatGPT was initially launched in November 2022 as a prototype that anyone could try online. It quickly gained popularity and attracted over 100 million users in the first month who wanted to chat with the AI. ChatGPT was built on top of an improved version of OpenAI's GPT-3 model, known as GPT-3.5, which was trained on a massive corpus of text data from the internet. GPT-3.5 is a generative pre-trained transformer (GPT) model, which means that it can generate coherent and diverse texts based on a few words or sentences of input.

In February 2023, GPT-4 was launched, offering yet again, tremendous improvements in speed, accuracy and factual correctness as well as its versatility and fluency of hundreds of languages. GPT-4 also offers the ability to analyse visual input, however, due to high computing intensity, this feature won't be rolled out to the public anytime soon.

The Technology behind ChatGPT

GPT models use a neural network architecture called transformers, which can learn the relationships between words and sentences in a text. ChatGPT was further fine-tuned using reinforcement learning from human feedback (RLHF), a technique that allows the model to learn from its own interactions with users and improve its performance over time.

ChatGPT also uses a dialogue format, which enables it to maintain context and coherence across multiple turns of conversation. ChatGPT can adapt to different domains and tasks with minimal or no fine-tuning, making it a versatile and powerful tool for natural language generation and understanding.

Applications & Use Cases

ChatGPT has many applications and use cases, such as:

- Content creation: ChatGPT can generate high-quality content for websites, blogs, or social media platforms in a few seconds. This includes creating content like product descriptions, blog posts, social media posts, drafts for business ideas, and long-form content like entire articles. ChatGPT can also help with creative writing applications, where it can generate unique ideas, brainstorm plots, and even write entire stories.

- Education: ChatGPT can help students learn new concepts, practice their skills, or test their knowledge by providing explanations, examples, quizzes, or feedback.

- Entertainment: It has the ability to entertain users by telling stories, jokes, riddles, or trivia, or by playing games such as 20 questions or hangman.

- Formating & Layouting: Feeling lazy? You can simply copy and paste your text into ChatGPT and ask it to format and layout the text for you. Using markup, it can make words or passages bold or italics, it can underline important sections or subdivide long text into paragraphs and bullet points as appropriate. Talk about useful!

- Information: The AI chatbot can provide users with information on various topics, such as history, science, geography, or current events, by answering questions or summarizing articles.

- Marketing: ChatGPT can generate marketing content that is catchy, persuasive, and tailored to the target audience. It is great at creating headlines, slogans, taglines, emails, landing pages, ads, and more.

- Writing code: ChatGPT can write code for simple or repetitive tasks, such as file I/O operations, data manipulation, and database queries. ChatGPT can also help with debugging, code completion, and code refactoring.

ChatGPT is definitely one of the most advanced and impressive examples of generative AI so far. In fact, it started the generative AI revolution! Only 6 months after its launch in December 2022, it has already amassed over 170 million users worldwide – and captured the imagination of AI developers and users worldwide. You can try ChatGPT now at chat.openai.com and see what it can do for you! (For a deeper dive, I recommend my book "ChatGPT for Beginners" which you can find on Amazon!).

Type	Text-to-Text
Price	Freemium, Free to use, ChatGPT Plus: 20 USD/month (exclusive access to plugins, GPT-4)
Link	https://chat.openai.com

10.2 Google Bard

Google Bard, a dialogue-based AI chatbot tool and ChatGPT competitor, utilizes Google's LaMDA (Language Model for Dialogue Applications) technology. Launched in Public Beta in May 2023, Bard remains experimental and employs LaMDA to facilitate interaction with generative AI.

Like ChatGPT, Google Bard is a conversational AI chatbot that can generate text of all kinds. You can ask it any question, as long as it doesn't violate its content policies, and Bard will provide an answer. You can also give it prompts to generate creative content, such as stories, poems, lyrics, jokes, or summaries.

Google Bard has some features and capabilities that make it different from other chatbots. For instance, it can generate multiple drafts of the same answer, and you can choose the one you like best or ask for new ones. It can also handle multiple topics and contexts in a single conversation, and switch between them seamlessly. It can also understand and use natural language expressions, such as metaphors, analogies, humor, and sarcasm.

How to use Google Bard (step-by-step)

1. Go to bard.google.com.
2. Sign in with your Google account and agree to the terms of service.
3. Type your input or question in the text box that says "Make an input here" and press enter or click on the arrow icon.
4. Wait for Bard to generate a response and two other drafts of the same response. You can click on "Show other drafts" to see them or click on "Regenerate drafts" to get new ones.

5. You can also edit your input by clicking on the pencil icon or delete it by clicking on the trash icon. You can also chat with other users or with the OpenAI bot by clicking on the chat icon.

6. You can scroll up and down to see your previous chats with Bard. They will be deleted when you close the window.

Here is a possible list of the top 7 tips for best results using Google Bard:

1. Be specific and clear with your input. Bard works best when you provide enough details and context for your query. For example, instead of typing "How to make pasta", you can type "How to make pasta with tomato sauce and cheese".

2. Use proper grammar and punctuation. Bard will try to match your style and tone, so if you use incorrect grammar or punctuation, it might affect the quality of the response. For example, instead of typing "whats ur name", you can type "What is your name?".

3. Avoid sensitive or inappropriate topics. Google has given its AI chatbot content policies that prevent it from generating responses that are harmful, abusive, hateful, violent, illegal, or otherwise objectionable. If you violate these policies, Bard might refuse to answer or give a warning message.

4. Experiment with different inputs and drafts. Bard can generate a variety of responses for the same input, so you can try different inputs and drafts to see what works best for you. You can also use different formats, such as bullet points, lists, tables, etc., to get different results.

5. Use Bard for creative purposes. Google Bard is not meant to be a source of factual information or a substitute for human judgment. It is a generative AI tool that can help you with creative tasks, such as writing stories, poems, lyrics, essays, summaries, etc. You can also use Bard for fun and entertainment, such as making jokes, riddles, trivia, etc.

6. Give feedback to Bard. Keep in mind that Bard is still an experimental tool that is constantly learning and improving. You can help Bard by giving feedback on its responses, such as rating them with stars or leaving comments. You can also report any bugs or issues that you encounter while using Bard.

7. Learn more about Bard and generative AI. Bard is based on Google's LaMDA (Language Model for Dialogue Applications), which is a breakthrough technology in natural language processing and generative AI. You can learn more about Bard and LaMDA by reading Google's blog posts, watching YouTube videos, or taking online courses on these topics.

Type	Text-to-Text

Price	Free for all
Link	https://bard.google.com

10.3 Claude 2 (by Anthropic)

Having been around since early 2023, it was in June 2023 with the release of Claude 2 that this powerful LLM and AI chatbot stole ChatGPT the show. In fact, many AI YouTubers heralded it as a "ChatGPT killer" and AITwitter went crazy over various unique features and capabilities that Claude 2 has over ChatGPT or Bard. While the truth is a little more nuanced, Claude 2 is an amazing alternative AI chatbot that most people still haven't heard of – and may not be able to use at this current point in time – as registrations are currently limited to the US and the UK.

What exactly is Claude 2?

Anthropic Claude 2 is a large language model that can generate text from natural language prompts, such as words, sentences, or paragraphs. It was developed by Anthropic, a research company that aims to create more reliable and beneficial artificial intelligence. The goal of Claude 2 is to help users with various tasks by providing them with natural language instructions and feedback.

History

Anthropic Claude 2 was first introduced in July 2023 and is only available for existing paid Anthropic users. To better understand the history of Claude 2, it is important to learn a little more about Anthropic itself:

Anthropic is a research company that aims to create more reliable and beneficial artificial intelligence. It was founded in 2021 by former senior members of OpenAI, who left the organization due to directional differences. Anthropic specializes in developing general AI systems and language models, with a company ethos of responsible AI usage. As of July 2023, Anthropic had raised US$1.5 billion in funding and was acquired by Google.

Anthropic's biggest project, a natural-language model named "Claude", is based on a technique called Constitutional AI, which aligns AI systems with human values and makes them helpful, harmless, and honest. Constitutional AI uses a set of principles to evaluate and improve the outputs of the AI system, without needing explicit human labels or oversight. Constitutional AI also uses constrained optimization techniques to make the AI system pursue helpfulness under its constitutional constraints, rather than seeking open-ended goals or optimization.

The goal of Constitutional AI is to create AI systems that proactively want to be helpful, harmless, and honest, and that align with ethics and human values without needing to be corralled or controlled through external systems. It's a technique focused on human benefit rather than pure capability.

The real USP for Claude 2 – at least as of August 2023 – is its impressive 100.000 token context window. This amazing feature allows the user to enter a text input of up to 70.000 words (such as entire 200–300-page books) and lets Claude 2 create outputs of up to 2.000-3.000 words in length. This is highly useful, e.g., if you want to summarize entire books or create a draft for an entire long-form blog post.

Applications & Use Cases

The applications and use cases of Claude 2 are basically identical with the text-based output tasks that ChatGPT can perform. It is inferior to ChatGPT in that there are no plugins for Claude 2 (at least as of August 2023; this might change with future plans). However, its prime feature – the 100.000 token context window – lends that AI chatbot perfect for usage in the following use cases:

- Text generation: The immense context window and high token limit also means that Claude 2 can output much longer texts than ChatGPT would (usually limited to 500-800 words at most). Why not let Claude 2 create drafts for entire reports or blog posts for you?
- Text summarization: Users can input up to around 70.000 words into Claude 2 and let it summarize or analyze the text for them; this feature can be very useful for both academic or professional research, market research and much more.

How to Use Anthropic Claude 2 (step-by-step)

1. Go to the Anthropic Claude 2 website at https://claude.ai.
2. Click on the "Talk to Claude" button and sign up for an account with your email and password.
3. Log in to your account and go to the Claude 2 panel on the left side of the workspace.
4. Enter your text prompt in the box and click on the Generate button. You can also use the Follow on Twitter feature to see more examples of Claude 2 content.
5. Wait for a few seconds and see the generated content below the box. You can also adjust the Length, Quality, and Diversity sliders to change the output settings.
6. If you are satisfied with the content, you can edit it further using the Anthropic tools or save it as a TXT file. You can also share it on social media platforms by clicking on the Share button.
7. You can repeat steps 4-6 as many times as you want with different text prompts.

Type	Text-to-Text
Price	Freemium model, free for all, Premium tiers without daily token

	limits
Link	https://claude.ai

10.4 Adobe Firefly

Adobe Firefly is a family of creative generative AI models that can create images from text prompts, such as words, sentences, or paragraphs. It is part of Adobe Sensei, Adobe's AI platform that powers various features and tools across Adobe products. The goal of Firefly is to help users expand their creativity and productivity by providing them with new ways to generate and edit content.

History

Adobe Firefly was first introduced in May 2023 and is only available for existing paid Adobe users. One of the features that made Adobe Firefly a real sensation is AutoFiller. AutoFiller is a feature that can automatically fill in the missing parts of an image based on the context and the text prompt. For example, if you have an image of a person with a missing arm, you can use AutoFiller to generate a realistic arm that matches the person's body and pose. AutoFiller can also generate backgrounds, foregrounds, and other elements that are missing or incomplete in an image.

Applications & Use Cases

Adobe Firefly has many applications and use cases, such as:

- Digital imaging and photography: Firefly can help users create and edit images by adding, extending, or removing content with simple text prompts.
- Illustration, artwork, and graphic design: Firefly can help users generate custom vectors, brushes, and textures from just a few words or even a sketch.
- Video: Firefly can help users change the mood, atmosphere, or even the weather of a video clip by describing what look they want.
- Marketing and social media: Firefly can help users create unique posters, banners, social posts, and more with a simple text prompt or by uploading a mood board.
- 3D modeling: Firefly can help users turn simple 3D compositions into photorealistic images and quickly create new styles and variations of 3D objects.

How to use Adobe Firefly (step-by-step)

1. Go to the Adobe Firefly website at https://www.adobe.com/sensei/generative-ai/firefly.html.
2. Click on the "Join the free beta" button and sign up for an account with your email and password.

3. Log in to your account and download the latest version of Photoshop from the Creative Cloud app.

4. Open Photoshop and go to the Firefly panel on the right side of the workspace.

5. Enter your text description in the box and click on the Generate button. You can also use the Follow on Instagram feature to see more examples of Firefly content.

6. Wait for a few seconds and see the generated content below the box. You can also adjust the Resolution, Quality, and Diversity sliders to change the output settings.

7. If you are satisfied with the content, you can edit it further using the Photoshop tools or save it as a PSD file. You can also share it on social media platforms by clicking on the Share button.

8. You can repeat steps 5-7 as many times as you want with different text descriptions.

Type	Text-to-Image, (Text-to-3D)
Price	Paid only, subscription of Adobe Photoshop required (~ 22 USD/month, ~ 250 USD/yr)
Link	Local, integrated into Adobe Photoshop/Creative Cloud

10.5 MidJourney

MidJourney is a generative AI tool that can create visually appealing images based on text prompts. The AI tool uses a variational autoencoder (VAE) to generate images that match the user's input as closely as possible.

History

The development company behind the AI tool, MidJourney, Inc. was founded in San Francisco, California by David Holz, who also co-founded Leap Motion, a motion control technology company. The MidJourney image generation platform first entered open beta on July 12, 2022, allowing anyone to join and try online. It quickly gained popularity and attracted over 100 million users in the first month.

The Technology

MidJourney was built from scratch with its own proprietary AI model that uses a variational autoencoder (VAE) model to generate images that match the user's input as closely as possible. The company has been releasing new model versions every few months with improved quality and diversity.

The latest version is 5.1, which adds more stylization and realism to the images. The previous versions are V1 (February 2022), V2 (April 12, 2022), V3 (July 25, 2022), V4 (November 5, 2022), and V5 (March 15, 2023).

MidJourney is currently only accessible through a Discord bot on their official Discord server, by direct messaging the bot, or by inviting the bot to a third party server. Users can type or choose a text input to generate images of various objects, scenes, animals, and abstract concepts.

They can also customize their images by adjusting the settings and parameters of the model. MidJourney is also working on a web interface.

Applications & Use Cases

Some of the features and capabilities of MidJourney text-to-image are:

- Users can generate images of various objects, scenes, animals, and even abstract concepts by typing a text description or choosing a preset. MidJourney will use its generative AI model to create an image that matches the user's input as closely as possible. The image will be generated in a grid of four thumbnails, each with a different variation

- Moreover, users have the ability to customize their images by adjusting the settings and parameters of the generative AI model, such as resolution, diversity, and quality.

  They can also view and compare different versions of the image by clicking on "Show other versions" or "Regenerate versions". They can also upscale the image to full quality by using additional credits

- With MidJourney, users may explore new image ideas and styles by browsing through the gallery of images created by other users or by the generative AI model itself. They can also search for images by keywords, categories, or filters. They can also rate and review the images they like or dislike.

- Other options for MidJourney users include exporting their images to their device or cloud storage, sharing their images with other users or platforms.

How to use MidJourney (step-by-step)

- Go to midjourney.com, sign up and join the MidJourney Online website or Discord server. You need a valid email address and a Discord account.

- Choose a subscription plan that suits your needs.

- Type your input or prompt in the text box starting "/imagine" and then entering your text prompt. You can be rather vague and let the model do the creative work for you, but more specific results including aspect ratio tend to deliver much better results.

- Wait for MidJourney to generate a preview with four possible drafts of your image. You can click on "Show other drafts" to see them or click on "Regenerate drafts" to get new ones.

- You can also edit your input by clicking on the pencil icon or delete it by clicking on the trash icon. You can also chat with other users or with the MidJourney bot by clicking on the chat icon.

- Choose one of the drafts that you like and click on "Finalize" to get the full-resolution image. You can also click on "Upscale" to get a higher-resolution image using the Upscaler Video model.
- You can scroll up and down to see your previous inputs and images with MidJourney. They will be saved in your account until you delete them.

Type	Text-to-Image, Text-to-Photo
Price	3 tiers: 10 USD, 30 USD, 60 USD/month
Link	https://midjourney.com

10.6 RunwayML

In July 2023, text-to-video was the biggest trend in the Generative AI scene – and created a lot of buzz on AI Twitter and among the Gen AI crowd. In all the hype around text-to-video and even image-to-video, one booming Gen AI tool took center stage: Runway ML.

What is Runway ML?

Runway ML is an online platform that enables anyone to use the power of artificial intelligence to create, edit, and transform images, videos, audio, and text. Runway ML offers dozens of so-called "AI magic tools" that can help you generate realistic and consistent videos with text, change the style of a video with text or images, create custom portraits, animals, styles and more, generate original images with nothing but words, transform any image with a text prompt, expand the edges of any image, turn a sequence of images into an animated video, erase and replace any part of any image, and much more. Runway ML also allows you to train your own custom models with your own data.

What Runway ML has gotten famous for, however, is its "Gen-2" text-to-video and image-to-video magic tools that have taken the AI world by storm – due to its ease of use and the impressive quality of the generated video outputs.

History

Runway ML was founded in 2018 by Cristóbal Valenzuela, Anastasis Germanidis, and Alejandro Matamala, who are artists and researchers with a passion for advancing creativity with artificial intelligence. They wanted to create a platform that would democratize access to AI and enable anyone to use it for creative purposes.

Runway ML was initially launched as a desktop application that connected to a cloud service. In 2020, Runway ML became a fully web-based platform that can run on any browser and device. Since then, Runway ML has grown to have over 300,000 users from over 150 countries and has been used by global brands, enterprises, and creatives to tell their stories.

Most important Runway ML features

While Runway ML has currently more than 30 "AI magic tools", it is these four important features that make it stand out and deserve the spot in the top Gen AI tools:

- Text-to-image: Similar to MidJourney, you can use RunwayML to create images based on your text prompts. You can also use the Text to Image tool to generate custom vectors, brushes, and textures from just a few words or even a sketch.

- Text-to-video: This is the real signature feature for RunwayML – and the one that made it take off. You can simply enter a text prompt and let RunwayML create an animated video for you.

  For example, if you have a text prompt of "a car driving on a highway at night", you can use RunwayML to generate a video that matches your description.

  You can also use the Video-to-Video tool to change the mood, atmosphere, or even the weather of a video clip by describing what look you want or uploading an image as an input.

- Image-to-video: Not only can RunwayML create videos for you based on text prompts, you can even use images as an additional input or simply upload any image and animate it with the respective Magic AI Tool.

  For example, if you have an image of a person and you want to make them move or dance, you can use RunwayML to generate a video that matches your vision.

  You can also use the Image to Video tool to animate any image with simple text prompts or by uploading a sound file as an input.

- 3D textures: This feature allows users to create and edit 3D models by generating realistic textures from text prompts or images. For example, if you have a text prompt of "a wooden table with scratches and stains", you can use RunwayML to generate a texture that matches your description.

Runway ML Applications & Use Cases

Runway ML can be used for various applications and use cases:

- Digital imaging and photography: RunwayML can help users create and edit images by adding, extending, or removing content with simple text prompts or images.

- Illustration, artwork, and graphic design: RunwayML can help users generate custom vectors, brushes, and textures from just a few words or even a sketch.

- Video: RunwayML can help users generate videos from text prompts or images, such as words, sentences, paragraphs, or photos. It can also transform existing videos into different styles or genres with simple text prompts or images.

- Marketing and social media: RunwayML can help users create unique posters, banners, social posts, and more with a simple text prompt or by uploading a mood board.

- 3D modeling: RunwayML can help users create and edit 3D models by generating realistic textures from text prompts or images. It can also turn simple 3D compositions into photorealistic images and quickly create new styles and variations of 3D objects.

How to Use Runway ML (Step-by-Step)

To use Runway ML, you need to follow these steps:

- Sign up for a free account on the official website of Runway ML: https://runwayml.com/. You will get 125 credits for free when you sign up.

- Choose one of the AI magic tools from the menu on the left side of the screen. You can browse by category or search by name.

- Follow the instructions on the screen to use the tool. You may need to upload your own data or choose from the available presets. You can also adjust the settings and parameters of the tool according to your needs.

- Click on the "Run" button to start the tool. You will see the results on the right side of the screen. You can also download or share the results with others.

- Repeat the process for other tools or projects as you wish.

Type	Text-to-Image, Text-to-Video, Image-to-Video
Price	Freemium model, premium tiers from 12-76 $ per month
Link	https://runwayml.com

10.7 GitHub Copilot

GitHub Copilot is a generative AI tool that can create code in various programming languages based on user inputs. Copilot is powered by OpenAI Codex, a neural network that can generate code with syntax, logic, and functionality, and even mimic the style of specific programmers.

Features & Capabilities

Some of the features and capabilities of GitHub Copilot are

- Code generation: CoPilot allows users to code by typing a text prompt or choosing a preset in their editor. The AI tool will use its generative AI model to create code that matches the user's input as closely as possible. The code will include syntax, logic, and functionality and be generated in the programming language of the user's choice.

- Code manipulation: Users can also manipulate existing code by typing a text prompt that specifies what they want to change or add to the code. GitHub Copilot will use its generative AI model to create new code that reflects the user's input as realistically as possible. Please note that the new code will be output in the same programming language as the original code.

- Code inspiration: Discovering new code ideas and styles by browsing through the gallery of code snippets created by other users or by the generative AI model itself is one of the exciting options the tool offers. Users may also search for code snippets by keywords, categories, or filters as well as rate and review the code snippets they like or dislike.

- Code execution: Users can use GitHub Copilot to execute their code directly from their editor. Highly practical, the AI tool integrates with various coding platforms and services, such as GitHub, Replit, CodePen, and more.

Want to test GitHub Copilot? Sign up for the beta program and install the GitHub Copilot extension in Visual Studio Code. Then you can start creating code with GitHub Copilot by typing or choosing your input in Visual Studio Code.

You might also edit their input by clicking on the pencil icon, or delete it by clicking on the trash icon. They can also chat with other users or with the OpenAI bot by clicking on the chat icon at https://docs.github.com/en/copilot/quickstart.

How to use GitHub Copilot (step-by-step)

Go to the GitHub Copilot website at https://github.com/features/copilot:

1. Click on the "Get early access" button and sign up for an account with your email and password.

2. Wait for an invitation email from GitHub to access GitHub Copilot. This may take some time as the product is in high demand and has limited availability.

3. Once you receive the invitation email, follow the instructions to install the GitHub Copilot extension for your preferred IDE. Currently, GitHub Copilot supports Visual Studio Code and Neovim.

4. To use GitHub Copilot, open your IDE and start typing your code or comments. You will see a suggested code completion in gray next to your cursor. You can accept the suggestion by pressing Tab or Enter, or ignore it by continuing to type.

5. You can also use the GitHub Copilot Playground interface on the GitHub website to try out different code suggestions without installing the extension. Go to https://copilot.github.com/playground and enter your natural language prompt or code snippet in the box. You will see a list of suggested code completions below the box.

6. You can repeat steps 5-6 as many times as you want with different code or comments.

Type	Text-to-Code
Price	For Individuals: 10 USD/month (100$/year), Business: 19 USD/month/user
Link	https://github.com/features/copilot

10.8 GenCraft

is an AI art generator tool that allows users to create stunning and personalized art photos and videos from a few words, using their imagination as a canvas. It harnesses a powerful AI model that can generate images and videos that match the user's as closely as possible. Users can also choose from a variety of styles input and genres to customize their creations.

GenCraft is easy to use and accessible across all devices - web, iOS, and Android. Smartphone users can also download and share their creations with the world. Overall, it is a fun and creative tool that can help users with various purposes and tasks, such as art, design, photography, marketing, education, and more.

Type	Text-to-Image, Text-to-Video
Price	Paid only, from 4 USD/month
Link	https://github.com/features/copilot

10.9 MusicLM

MusicLM by Google is an experimental text to music model that can generate unique songs based on user's ideas or descriptions. The text-to-music tool was introduced by Google in May 2023 as part of their Generative AI announcements at IO. Users can sign up to try MusicLM in AI Test Kitchen on the web, Android or iOS. Users can type in a prompt like "soulful jazz for a dinner party" and MusicLM will create two versions of the song for them. Simply listen to both and give feedback to the model. Overall, this is still a rather simple tool but it offers a preview of more advanced text-to-music AI tools bound to be released in the coming months.

Type	Text-to-Music
Price	Free for all

Link	https://aitestkitchen.withgoogle.com/experiments/music-lm

10.10 Generative AI Tools - Epilogue

There you have it – the most promising and powerful generative AI solutions at present. Keep in mind that this list is very short and could have been extended by many apps. Also note, of course, that this list might be outdated soon as new powerful AI tools – be it text-to-text, text-to-image, text-to-video, etc. – are released onto the market.

Was there a particular AI tool that sounded particularly exciting or interesting to you? If so, I strongly urge you to go and try it out now. Yes, even if it is a paid one! Get a 1-month-subscription and start playing around. It is really the best thing you can do. Other than reading this book and learning all about generative AI :) – there is nothing like practical experience. You are going to have a lot of aha-moments and start to become more proficient in generative AI.

As it has been said "You are not going to be replaced by AI, you are going to be replaced by a human using AI." Don't be that person!

CHAPTER 11: HOW GENERATIVE AI WILL TRANSFORM SPECIFIC INDUSTRIES

Having developed a strong understanding of Generative AI and its technical underpinnings, and the top consumer tools, we are now ready to examine how generative AI is set to transform various industries.

In Chapter 11, we explore the potential impacts of Generative AI on sectors such as Healthcare, Entertainment, Fashion and Retail, Architecture and Design, the Automotive industry, Agriculture and Food production, Education, and Journalism and Media. The wide range of industries touched upon in this chapter underscores the versatility and transformative potential of Generative AI.

11.1 Healthcare

The intersection of generative AI and healthcare holds promise to significantly alter the way care is provided and treatments are developed. Generative AI models can leverage large amounts of data and generate novel and useful outputs, such as drug compounds, treatment plans, and medical images. These outputs can help in improving the efficiency, accuracy, and personalization of healthcare services. In this chapter, we will explore some of the applications and benefits of generative AI in the healthcare industry.

11.1.1 Drug Discovery

Generative AI is an absolute game changer in the discovery of new drugs, a process that involves identifying new substances with potential medicinal value for disease treatment. Traditionally, it has been an intricate, lengthy, and costly procedure that requires creating and testing millions of compounds. However, generative AI models can streamline this process by generating possible drug compounds and assessing their effectiveness.

There are multiple ways in which generative AI can help in this process:

AI-enabled Molecular Design

The application of domain-specific generative AI models can bring about the production of innovative molecular structures with a high likelihood of being effective therapeutic drugs, thus minimizing time and cost. For instance, the AI model could take a target protein or disease as an input and generate molecules that could bind to or inhibit that protein or disease. These molecules are then further examined and refined by experts or other AI models.

Predictive Abilities

Generative AI models can leverage existing molecular structure databases and their properties to forecast the biological activity of new drug compounds. This process aids in initial screening, reducing the number of compounds that require synthesis and physical testing. A respective model could take a new molecule as input and predict its pharmacokinetic and pharmacodynamic properties, toxicity, and potential side effects.

11.1.2 Personalized Medicine

Another way generative AI creates value is by contributing to personalized medicine, which tailors medical treatments based on each patient's unique characteristics, including genetic makeup, medical history, lifestyle, and preferences. This individualized approach can enhance treatment effectiveness and safety, preventing unnecessary or harmful interventions.

With its data analysis and insight generation capabilities, generative AI is instrumental in creating tailored treatment plans. It aids personalized medicine in the following ways:

Genomics and Custom Treatment Plans

AI can scrutinize a patient's genetic data along with their medical history to produce personalized treatment plans. It has the potential to anticipate how a patient will react to specific medications, enabling doctors to tailor treatments.

One potential example is that a generative model might take a patient's genomic sequence as input and generate a list of likely effective or ineffective drugs for their condition.

Lifestyle Recommendations

Generative AI is able to utilize data about a patient's lifestyle, including diet, physical activity, sleep habits, stress levels, and environmental factors, to offer tailored recommendations to improve overall health and prevent disease. By feeding the generative AI model with a patient's lifestyle data as input, it can produce a set of suggestions to enhance nutrition, physical activity, sleep quality, and mental health.

11.1.3 Medical Imaging

Medical imaging entails creating visual representations of the body's internal structures or functions for clinical analysis and diagnosis, including methods like X-rays, ultrasound, CT scans, MRIs, and PET scans. Generative AI offers substantial opportunities in this area, including synthesizing images, identifying anomalies, and enabling 3D reconstructions. Here is how generative AI aids in medical imaging:

Production of Synthetic Medical Images

Particularly GAN-based generative AI models are capable of producing synthetic medical images resembling actual patient data. These images enhance the diagnostic capabilities of other AI models and medical professionals, without violating the privacy of any patients. As an example, a generative model can utilize a text description or a sketch as input and produce a realistic corresponding medical image.

Anomaly Detection

AI can identify anomalies or irregularities in medical scans, such as tumors in MRI scans or lesions in X-rays and thereby be a great support for radiologists in their evaluations. A respectively trained generative AI model can analyze a medical image as input, emphasize areas likely to contain an anomaly, or create a report detailing the anomaly.

3D Reconstruction

Generative AI can transform 2D medical images into 3D models, assisting surgeons in pre-operative planning and enhancing visualizations for medical education. AI models could be leveraged to process a sequence of 2D images as input and generate a 3D model of the organ or tissue being imaged.

11.2 Entertainment

The entertainment sector stands to benefit substantially from generative AI, as it can revolutionize content creation and consumption. By processing extensive data, generative AI produces novel content such as music, dialogues, environments, and narratives, enhancing content quality, diversity, and personalization.

11.2.1 Music

Generative AI can bring enormous changes to the music industry as it offers the ability to automate the creation of music across various genres and styles. Here are some of its possible applications:

Composition Assisted by AI

AI models, like OpenAI's MuseNet, generate unique compositions across styles, ranging from classical to pop. Musicians can utilize these AI-generated compositions as a creative springboard. A possible example is that AI can generate a melody or chord progression per the musician's preference, which can be further developed using their own instruments or vocals.

Customized Music Generation

Another change AI brings to the music industry is the generation of music experiences tailored to listeners. Based on listeners' preferences and behaviors, AI can generate music tracks specifically suited to individual tastes. How might this look? For example, an AI model could generate a playlist complementing the listener's mood, activity, or location, or even create new songs inspired by their favorite artists or genres.

11.2.2 Film and Video Games

Filmmaking and video game development could be completely transformed by adequate generative AI models that could over tasks like the creation of dialogues, responsive environments, and narratives. Here is how this could look:

AI-Generated Dialogues

AI models can create dialogues for characters in films and video games, enhancing realism and the storyline. An AI model can consider a character's personality, background, and emotion to generate suitable dialogues based on the context. Even a general-purpose LLM model like ChatGPT does a really impressive job at this.

Responsive Game Environments

Generative AI can create adaptive and dynamic game environments that respond to player's actions, offering more immersive gameplay. An AI model can generate diverse scenarios or outcomes contingent on player's choices, creating a branching narrative with multiple potential paths.

AI-Based Storytelling

AI can generate comprehensive narratives and thereby redefine the current process of story development in films and games. An AI model could take a genre, theme, or plot as input and generate an engaging story, complete with characters, settings, events, and conflicts.

11.2.3 Virtual Reality

Generative AI can also elevate Virtual Reality (VR), a technology enabling interaction with simulated environments through devices like headsets or controllers. Here's how:

Virtual World Generation

Domain-specific AI models could create complex, lifelike virtual worlds for VR, capable of dynamic responses to user actions for an immersive experience. An AI model can generate a virtual city complete with buildings, streets, cars, people, and weather, all responsive to user's movements and actions.

Filling VR Environments

AI can populate these virtual worlds with AI-generated characters and objects that interact with the user in real-time, enhancing immersion and engagement. An example could be an AI model that generates realistic human faces and voices for virtual characters, enabling them to converse with the user or perform tasks.

While generative AI can elevate entertainment content, its development and use should be responsible, considering challenges and risks such as ethical, legal, and social implications, data quality and security, and human-AI interaction issues. It is vital to ensure alignment with human values and goals.

11.3 Fashion and Retail

As you are going to discover in this chapter, generative AI has the potential to significantly influence the fashion and retail industry, from enhancing the shopping experience to improving inventory management. It can help fashion companies to enhance their creativity, efficiency and customer experience in various ways:

11.3.1 Personalized Shopping

By tailoring products and services to individual customers, generative AI can provide a more personalized and engaging shopping experience.

Custom-Designed Products

Generative AI models can design custom products based on customer preferences and styles. For instance, an AI could take into account a customer's past purchases, preferred styles, and sizes to create a unique piece of clothing or accessory. This can increase customer satisfaction and loyalty, as well as differentiate the brand from competitors.

Some examples of companies using generative AI for custom-designed products are:

- **Stitch Fix**: Operating as an internet-based personal style service, Stitch Fix employs generative AI to generate tailored outfits for its clientele, considering their unique style profiles, feedback, and predilections. The enterprise blends the expertise of human stylists with advanced algorithms to assemble collections of clothes and accessories that align with the client's personal taste, budget constraints, and specific events.

- **The Fabricant**: Renowned as a virtual fashion establishment, The Fabricant leverages generative AI to produce bespoke digital attire. Utilizing 3D design software and Generative Adversarial Networks (GANs), the company crafts lifelike and expressive digital outfits that can either be flaunted in virtual realms or overlaid on imagery or video content.

- **Zalora**: Zalora, an online fashion commerce platform, exploits generative AI to offer personalized product suggestions to its shoppers. By employing a sophisticated deep learning model, StyleGAN, the company generates visuals of products that harmonize with the customer's stylistic choices, which are derived from their browsing patterns, purchasing habits, and feedback.

Personalized Recommendations

AI can analyze customer data to understand shopping habits and preferences and generate personalized product recommendations. This targeted approach can enhance the customer experience and increase sales by providing relevant and timely suggestions that suit the customer's needs and wants. Some examples of companies using generative AI for personalized recommendations are:

- **Amazon**: As an e-commerce behemoth, Amazon leverages generative AI to furnish personalized product suggestions for its user base. Amazon employs a sophisticated deep learning model named DeepAR, which generates precise demand predictions for individual items, factoring in historical sales data, customer feedback, ratings, and other determinants. These projections subsequently aid in ranking and suggesting products that are most likely to resonate with each customer.

- **Revolve**: Revolve, an online fashion commerce platform, capitalizes on generative AI to fabricate personalized marketing visuals for its clientele. The enterprise relies on an advanced deep learning model, StyleGAN2, to create images of models donning ensembles that align with the customer's style preferences, inferred from their browsing history, purchasing habits, and feedback. These visuals are subsequently utilized to construct tailored emails, advertisements, and social media content that highlight products the customer might find appealing.

- **Prada Beauty**: Prada Beauty, a high-end beauty brand, employs generative AI to produce custom-tailored product recommendations for its customers. Utilizing a deep learning model named CycleGAN, the company generates images of customers flaunting various lipstick shades, based on their uploaded selfies. These images are then analyzed to suggest the most fitting lipstick color for each customer, considering their skin tone, hair color, and personal fashion sense.

11.3.2 Inventory Management and Demand Forecasting

Generative AI can improve inventory management and demand forecasting, helping retailers optimize their operations.

Predicting Demand

AI models can scrutinize sales statistics, market tendencies, and other variables to generate precise demand predictions. These estimations can aid retailers in making insightful decisions regarding which products to stock and the desired quantity, as well as planning for seasonal fluctuations, promotional events, and other activities. This can enhance operational effectiveness, minimize inventory expenditures, and prevent lost sales due to understocking or overstocking.

Examples of businesses utilizing generative AI for demand prediction include:

- **H&M**: Operating as a worldwide fashion retailer, H&M utilizes generative AI to anticipate demand for its offerings across varied markets and platforms. The company employs a deep learning model, LSTM, to evaluate historical sales data, customer behavior, climatic conditions, and other factors to generate demand forecasts for each product and outlet. These forecasts subsequently aid in optimizing inventory allocation, replenishment, and pricing strategies.

- **Nike**: Recognized as a prominent sportswear label, Nike leverages generative AI to predict product demand and enhance its supply chain. The company relies on a deep learning model, Seq2Seq, to examine sales data, customer feedback, social media, and other variables to generate demand forecasts for each product and region. These predictions then guide the planning of production, distribution, and marketing strategies.

- **Adidas**: As a global sportswear label, Adidas employs generative AI to anticipate product demand and formulate customized offers for its customers. Adidas utilizes a deep learning model, Transformer, to scrutinize sales data, customer predilections, and other factors to generate demand estimates for each product and customer segment. These predictions subsequently assist in customizing product assortments, pricing, and promotional activities for each customer.

Optimizing Inventory

Enhanced demand forecasting allows retailers to refine their inventory management, reducing instances of surplus stock and stockouts. This not only curtails wastage and costs but also guarantees that customers can locate their desired items when needed. Some instances of businesses using generative AI for inventory optimization include:

- **Zara**: Known as a leader in the fast-fashion industry, Zara makes use of AI models to fine-tune its inventory control and minimize wastage. Zara employs a sophisticated deep learning model, VAE, to scrutinize sales statistics, customer feedback, among other variables, and to determine the ideal inventory levels for every product and store. These levels subsequently influence alterations in production, distribution, and restocking strategies.

- **Walmart**: As the world's largest brick-and-mortar retail giant, Walmart uses generative AI to optimize its inventory management and improve customer service. The company relies on an advanced deep learning model, GAN, to analyze sales figures, customer predilections, and other relevant data.

11.4 Architecture and Design

Generative AI is significantly influencing the architecture and design industry, creating new opportunities and capabilities for design innovation. Generative AI is an iterative process that uses AI technology and evolutionary algorithms to suggest a range of solutions that meet certain criteria. It can also simulate and analyze the performance of each solution against predefined criteria, such as functionality, aesthetics, cost, and environmental impact. Generative AI is transforming how architects and designers approach their work, offering a new way to explore a vast range of design possibilities.

11.4.1 Generative Design in Architecture

Generative AI is transforming how architects and designers approach their work, offering a new way to explore a vast range of design possibilities. Generative AI can create innovative solutions that human designers may not have considered, optimizing the design process. It can also evaluate how well a design will hold up under different weather conditions, how efficiently it uses space, or how much it will cost to build.

Design Optimization

Generative AI models can create a multitude of design alternatives based on specific input parameters such as available space, material type, budget, and environmental considerations. These AI-generated options can provide innovative solutions that human designers may not have considered, optimizing the design process. For example, generative AI was used to design the Autodesk Toronto office, which resulted in a 25% reduction in material use and a 50% reduction in construction time.

Simulation and Analysis

In addition to generating design options, AI can also simulate and analyze each option's performance against predefined criteria. For instance, it can evaluate how well a design will hold up under different weather conditions, how efficiently it uses space, or how much it will cost to build. This allows for the comparison and selection of the best design option based on the desired outcomes. Want an example? Already in 2008, a very rudimentary AI model was used to design the Beijing National Stadium for the 2008 Olympics, which simulated the structural stability and wind resistance of various designs.

11.4.2 Generative Design in Product Development

Generative AI is finding its way into product development, empowering designers to craft more inventive, efficient, and custom-tailored products. The technology is capable of producing a myriad of product designs, taking into account particular constraints such as material composition, cost, and functionality. Moreover, it can create personalized designs that cater to the unique preferences of each customer.

Product Optimization

Similar to its use in architecture, generative AI can can churn out a variety of product designs considering specific limitations such as the materials used, the cost involved, and the functionality. This enables the exploration of a broader set of possibilities and assists in identifying optimized solutions. As an instance, generative AI was instrumental in designing a lightweight bicycle frame that resulted in a material usage reduction by 18% and an increase in strength by 20%.

Personalized Products

Domain-specific AI models can deliver customized designs that align with individual consumer preferences. For example, a company specializing in furniture could leverage AI to generate tailor-made furniture designs rooted in a customer's specific requirements and aesthetic inclinations. This could boost customer satisfaction and loyalty by delivering distinctive and personalized products.

Given its proficiency in quickly and efficiently navigating a vast design landscape, generative AI is poised to revolutionize the way we approach design and architecture, leading to more innovative and customized solutions.

11.5 Automotive Industry

Generative AI can radically transform the automotive industry, providing innovative solutions in design, manufacturing, and autonomous driving.

11.5.1 Design and Manufacturing

By reshaping how cars are designed and manufactured, generative AI can lead to greater efficiency and cost savings for manufacturers and suppliers:

Generative Design

Leveraging the power of AI in generative design can aid in producing lightweight yet durable car components. Designers can input constraints such as weight, strength, material, and fabrication techniques into the AI to produce an array of optimized designs. This strategy can yield considerable cost reductions and performance enhancements. For instance, General Motors harnessed generative design to engineer a novel seat bracket that lessened weight by 40% and cut part count by 80%

Streamlined Manufacturing

AI can also be instrumental in refining the manufacturing process. By anticipating potential hitches in the assembly line or optimizing the arrangement of parts for efficient assembly, AI can reduce downtime and augment production efficiency. As an example, BMW employs an AI system to monitor the quality of its welding operations and identify flaws in real time.

11.5.2 Autonomous Driving

Generative AI plays a critical role in the development and functioning of autonomous vehicles.

Sensor Data Interpretation

Being able to decipher intricate sensor data, generative AI algorithms enable the car to comprehend its environment. AI systems process information from Lidar, radar, and cameras to build an intricate 3D map of the surroundings, identifying other vehicles, pedestrians, and obstacles. Tesla, for instance, uses a neural network to process images from eight surrounding cameras and generate a comprehensive 360-degree perspective of the vehicle's surroundings.

Decision Making

Beyond merely interpreting the environment, generative AI also plays a pivotal role in decision-making for autonomous driving. These systems can formulate appropriate driving actions based on the analyzed sensor data and established driving protocols. Tasks include maintaining lanes, avoiding obstacles, and executing complex maneuvers like merging onto highways or navigating intersections. Waymo, for example, uses a reinforcement learning algorithm to train its self-driving cars to navigate challenging situations like unprotected left turns or roundabouts.

Incorporating generative AI into the automotive industry has the potential to propel substantial advancements, particularly in vehicle design, manufacturing efficiency, and the shift towards fully autonomous vehicles.

11.6 Agriculture and Food Production

Generative AI has the potential to bring about a paradigm shift in the agricultural sector and food production, leading to increased efficiency, sustainability, and innovation.

11.6.1 Crop Optimization

AI models have already proven to be invaluable tools in optimizing crop growth, leading to improved yields and sustainability – ultimately contributing towards reducing global hunger and malnourishment.

Predictive Agriculture

Consider that generative AI is capable of deriving optimal planting configurations and timelines considering numerous factors like weather patterns, soil health, pest presence, crop variety, and other environmental aspects. Such predictive models aid farmers in making insightful decisions regarding the timing and location of planting, which leads to improved crop yields and minimized wastage.

Precision Farming

AI can also contribute to precision farming, where resources such as water, fertilizers, and pesticides are utilized more efficiently. By forecasting the precise requirements of plants at varying stages of their growth and under different weather scenarios, AI can ensure that crops receive exactly what they need, exactly when they need it. This results in reducing overuse and mitigating environmental impact.

11.6.2 Food Innovation

Generative AI is pioneering new avenues in food innovation, ranging from the creation of novel recipes to predicting consumer preferences.

Recipe Creation

Generative AI models have the capacity to conjure new and enticing recipes by assembling ingredients in unique combinations. These AI systems can learn from extensive databases of existing recipes and generate novel combinations, potentially leading to culinary breakthroughs.

Flavor Combination and Personalized Nutrition

In the same vein, AI can generate distinct flavor pairings, resulting in the creation of innovative food products. Additionally, by deciphering an individual's dietary preferences and nutritional needs, AI could potentially generate personalized meal plans and nutritional advice, leading to enhanced health outcomes.

> Generative AI is transforming agriculture and food production in multifaceted ways. With its capabilities to optimize crop growth and foster food creation innovation, AI promises to elevate the quality and quantity of the food supply in the near future.

11.7 Education

The education sector also stands to profit in numerous ways from the application of generative AI models with possible use cases like the creation of personalized learning experiences, adaptive assessments, and generating interactive learning materials.

11.7.1 Personalized Learning

Personalized educational content and learning experiences create more student engagement and thereby help to improve their learning success and retention. With generative AI, it is finally possible to create personalized educational content for each student – easily and effectively at scale.

Adaptive Content Generation

AI models can generate learning content that adapts to each student's learning style, pace, and level of understanding. For example, if a student struggles with a particular concept, the AI can generate additional material or exercises focused on that concept to aid understanding. This can enhance the learning process by providing customized and relevant content.

Individual Learning Pathways

Through the analysis of student's performance and learning patterns over time, generative AI can create individual learning pathways. These pathways can guide a student's learning journey, suggesting what to learn next or identifying areas where more practice is needed. As it provides personalized and optimal guidance, this would improve learning outcomes of the majority of students.

11.7.2 Adaptive Assessments

Adaptive assessments offer a better gauge a student's understanding and progress, yet teachers and public schools simply don't have the time or resources to; generative AI solves this, allowing for adaptive assessments for all students or classes as needs change.

Test Generation

AI can generate quizzes or tests tailored to a student's current level, focusing on areas that need improvement. This adaptive testing approach can provide a more accurate picture of a student's comprehension and progress than traditional standardized tests. Another benefit would be a lower test anxiety and increased motivation by providing appropriate challenges and feedback.

11.7.3 Interactive Learning Experiences

Generative AI can also contribute to creating engaging and interactive learning experiences.

AI Tutors

AI could generate interactive, AI-powered learning experiences that simulate one-on-one tutoring. These AI tutors can provide immediate feedback, answer questions, and provide explanations, enhancing the learning experience. They can also adapt to the student's needs and preferences, creating a personalized and supportive learning environment.

> Generative AI holds the promise of making education more personalized, adaptive, and engaging, potentially transforming how students learn and how educators teach. As AI technology continues to advance, its role in education is likely to expand even further."

11.8 Journalism and Media

Another industry that stands to be disrupted by generative AI is journalism and media, as powerful AI models provide tools for drafting articles, analyzing data, creating visual representations, and speeding up the content creation process.

Here is how these applications break down:

11.8.1 Article Drafting

Generative AI can expedite the content creation process by drafting articles. Here, AI can use provided keywords or topics to generate rough drafts, which human journalists can then refine. This allows journalists to focus more on investigative work and crafting the narrative, while AI handles the more routine aspect of initial drafting. Not only amateur copywriters using ChatGPT for their landing pages or email newsletters do this. For example, the world-class journalistic organisation Reuters uses an AI tool called Lynx Insight to generate story ideas and headlines based on data analysis.

11.8.2 Data Analysis and Visualization

AI can play a crucial role in handling large datasets, a common challenge in today's data-driven journalism. AI tools can quickly analyze and draw conclusions from vast amounts of data, making it easier for journalists to spot trends, correlations, and notable insights. Additionally, it could generate data visualizations, transforming complex datasets into compelling, easily digestible graphics. For instance, The New York Times employs the AI tool "Perspective" that produces interactive charts and maps based on user input.

11.8.3 Automated Content Generation

Beyond drafting articles and analyzing data, AI can generate a variety of content types autonomously. As an example, AI writes social media updates, generate headlines, or even write short news pieces for specific sections like sports or finance. This can significantly improve the speed and scale of content production, particularly for online media outlets. Want an example? The Washington Post has its own AI tool called "Heliograf" that generates automated stories on topics such as election results or high school sports.

> By enhancing productivity and enabling more data-driven reporting, generative AI could facilitate a new era of journalism that blends human creativity with machine efficiency. However, it also presents new ethical considerations, such as ensuring AI-generated content's accuracy and managing the potential displacement of certain journalism roles.

11.9 Hiring and Recruiting

Generative AI can improve and streamline the hiring and recruiting process for corporations tremendously, helping them to deal with the ever-growing pressures of talent shortages, diversity and inclusion goals, remote work arrangements, and increasing expectations by the candidates themselves.

Writing Job Ads and Candidate Communications

One of the tasks generative AI will take over is writing job ads and conducting candidate communications. This can save time and effort for hiring managers who may not have the skills or resources to craft effective and engaging messages. ChatGPT is a amazing when it comes to writing copy like cover letters, CVs, emails, or social media ads. Candidates can use ChatGPT to generate personalized and professional content that showcases their skills and achievements. Hiring managers can also use ChatGPT to write job descriptions that attract quality candidates for a role.

Companies can also use ChatGPT to translate their job ads into non-native language, which can be useful for global or multilingual recruitment – but of course they should be checked by trained linguists before publication. Moreover, generative AI can help avoid biases and stereotypes in job ads and candidate communications by using inclusive and neutral language or giving feedback on existing job ads.

Sourcing and Assessing Candidates

Another task that generative AI can assist with is sourcing and assessing candidates. This can help recruiters find the best talent for their roles faster and easier (meaning cheaper and more reliably).

For instance, HireBee is a generative AI platform that uses natural language processing and computer vision to analyze job descriptions and resumes. It can then generate a list of qualified candidates based on their skills, experience, and fit for the role. HireBee can also generate customized assessments and interview questions for each candidate based on their profile.

Generative AI can also help recruiters source candidates from diverse backgrounds and underrepresented groups by expanding their reach and visibility. As an example, Datapeople is a generative AI tool that can create targeted job ads for different demographics and platforms. Moreover, Datapeople allows for the optimization of the ads for search engines and social media algorithms to increase their exposure.

Enhancing the Candidate Experience

Speaking very generally, generative AI can improve and enhance the overall candidate experience. This can help recruiters build trust and rapport with candidates and increase their satisfaction and engagement.

Want an example? Impress is a generative AI chatbot that can interact with candidates throughout the hiring process. It can answer their questions, provide feedback, schedule interviews, or send reminders, but also personalize the conversation based on the candidate's preferences and behavior.

Generative AI may also help recruiters provide a more human touch to the candidate experience by using natural language generation and emotional intelligence. For example, LinkedIn is testing new AI-powered job descriptions that can generate tailored messages for each candidate based on their profile and interests.

The Future of Generative AI in Hiring

Using generative AI in the hiring process still has its challenges and limitations. Generative AI may, for instance, produce inaccurate or misleading content that could harm the reputation or credibility of recruiters or candidates. It may also raise ethical or legal issues regarding data privacy, consent, or ownership. Thus, complete automation seems unlikely in the current field as hiring managers, legal department, etc. still have to review and sign off on generated job ads and candidate communication.

Therefore, generative AI should not replace human judgment or interaction in hiring but rather complement it. Generative AI should be used as a tool to augment human capabilities and creativity, not to automate them entirely. Recruiters should always verify the information and edit the content generated by generative AI before using it. They have to monitor the performance and impact of generative AI on their hiring outcomes and candidate experience.

11.10 Sales

The sales industry will also be transformed by the power of generative AI as it helps them to find creative and better solutions to challenges like ever-growing competition, changing customer expectations, rising costs, and regulatory complexity.

Here are some of the tasks generative AI can already take over or at least facilitate:

Writing Sales Emails and Pitches

One of the tasks that generative AI can automate is writing sales emails and pitches. This can save time and effort for sales representatives who may not have the skills or resources to craft effective and engaging messages. Most certainly, you have already seen for yourself how proficient ChatGPT is in writing copy like personalized emails, tailored pitches, or follow-up messages.

Sales representatives can use ChatGPT to generate customized and professional content that showcases their value proposition and builds rapport with prospects or to write sales emails and pitches that attract quality leads for their products or services. Virtually all kinds of copywriting can be done with ChatGPT or more particular GPT-4-based tools, such that sales reps have more time to focus on understanding the needs of their customers and leads and close more leads in less time.

Sourcing and Assessing Leads

Generative AI tools can also be used to assist with sourcing and assessing leads so that sales reps can identify the most qualified prospects for their products or services faster and easier.

Market leader HubSpot has already implemented a generative AI platform that uses NLP and computer vision to analyze customer profiles and preferences. It can then generate a list of qualified leads based on their needs, goals, and fit for the product or service. HubSpot can also generate customized recommendations and reminders for each lead based on their profile.

Generative AI can also help sales representatives source leads from diverse backgrounds and underrepresented groups by expanding their reach and visibility. For example, LawGeex is a generative AI tool that can create targeted ads for different demographics and platforms.

Enhancing the Customer Experience

Talking more generally, generative AI can help organizations to drastically improve and upgrade the customer experience. This can help sales representatives build trust and rapport with customers and increase their satisfaction and retention.

For example, Viva Sales is a generative AI chatbot that can interact with customers throughout the sales process. It can answer their questions, provide feedback, schedule meetings, or send reminder as well as personalize the conversation based on the customer's preferences and behavior. Meanwhile, Salesforce is testing new AI-powered chatbots that can generate tailored messages for each customer based on their profile and interests.

The Future of Generative AI in Sales

Put simply: Generative AI can be extremely useful in sales but it does present various problems. It might generate false or misleading content that could damage reputations and possibly lead to privacy, consent, or ownership issues. It should supplement human judgment in sales, not replace it. It's important for sales reps to verify and edit AI-generated content, and to monitor its effect on sales results and customer experience.

11.11 Law Services

The law firm model is changing – due to generative AI! Yes, generative AI could even replace or certainly assist and augment the role of traditional lawyers in various ways. Let's explore some of the ways in which generative AI is going to make its strides in the legal world.

Researching and Writing Legal Documents

Already some law firms are using GPT-4-based tools to automate researching and writing legal documents – a real time-saver for overworked or uncreative lawyers who may not have the skills or resources to craft effective and engaging documents.

Tools like ChatGPT can be used to create drafts for all kinds of written documents like contracts, memos, briefs, or opinions. Lawyers can use ChatGPT to generate personalized and professional content that showcases their arguments and evidence. Law firms can also use ChatGPT to write legal documents that attract quality clients for their services. Naturally, these documents can only be used as a first draft and have to be reviewed and edited by lawyers and law professionals to ensure consistency, compliance, factual correctness and relevance for the applying law.

Generative AI can also help lawyers research legal issues and precedents by using natural language processing and information retrieval. A popular example is Thomson Reuters Westlaw Edge, a generative AI tool that can analyze legal questions and generate relevant answers and citations. It can also optimize the documents for search engines and legal databases to increase their exposure.

Sourcing and Assessing Client

Generative AI can help law firms find and evaluate clients more quickly and easily. For example, LexisNexis InterAction, an AI platform, analyzes client profiles and creates a list of suitable clients for a firm. Also, tools like LawGeex can increase a firm's reach to clients from diverse backgrounds through targeted ads.

Enhancing the Client Experience

Furthermore, AI can improve client experience. AI chatbots like ROSS Intelligence can interact with clients, answer their questions, and send reminders, personalizing their interactions based on client preferences.

However, using generative AI tools in law firms has its downsides. It can generate misleading content and may present ethical or legal issues around privacy and consent. These tools should be used to enhance, not replace human judgment. Lawyers need to verify AI-generated information and monitor its effect on their cases and client satisfaction. Despite these issues, generative AI presents vast potential for law firms, combining the power of AI and human expertise to make decisions and provide better services.

11.12 Personal Sports Coaching

While this industry is barely ever talked about in the context of AI, generative AI can help to transform the personal sports coaching process in various ways. Let's explore how:

Generating personalized training and diet plans

Generative AI can use data from athletes' performance, health, and preferences to create customized and optimal training and diet plans for each individual. This can help athletes improve their skills, fitness, and well-being. A great example is V7 AI, an AI platform that analyzes video footage of athletes and generates feedback and suggestions on how to improve their technique, posture, and movement.

Generating self-coaching chatbots

Providing support on specific topics or goals, generative AI can create chatbots that act as a simulated coach. This technology allows athletes to receive coaching anytime, improving their resilience, motivation, and confidence. An example of this is a project by Rebecca Rutschmann, a former professional athlete, who is developing a generative AI chatbot to offer self-coaching on common coaching issues.

Generating game strategies and tactics

By using data from past games and opponents, generative AI can formulate game plans and tactics. This capability assists coaches and players in their preparation for diverse situations, anticipation of obstacles, and performance enhancement. A case in point is Infront, an AI platform, which interprets game data to provide insights and advice for players and coaches.

Generating game highlights and summaries

Generative AI can produce game highlights and summaries using statistical data and video footage from games. These summaries and highlights help players and coaches to evaluate their performance, understand their strengths and weaknesses, and learn from their errors. Additionally, sports entities can use generative AI to generate game highlights and summaries, as facilitated by platforms like Infront.

The Future of Generative AI in Professional Sports Coaching

While generative AI has potential in professional sports coaching, it is not without its limitations. These limitations can include the generation of misleading or inaccurate content, which can potentially harm the reputation of athletes or coaches. Furthermore, the technology might lead to ethical or legal issues surrounding consent, data privacy, or ownership.

11.13 How Generative AI Will Transform Specific Industries – Epilogue

We've covered a lot of ground in this chapter, exploring how Generative AI can have an impact across various industries, from healthcare to journalism. This technology can provide new solutions and opportunities. The examples we've looked at give a glimpse of the possible applications and benefits of Generative AI. Hopefully, they've made you think about how you can use this technology effectively in your own field or context.

However, we still have more to discuss. In the final part of this book, we're going to address some important considerations around Generative AI. We'll discuss the ethical issues that come with using this technology and how we might navigate them. Moreover, we will take a look at the best resources, AI influences and thought leaders that are going to help you to stay on top and have an edge over your competition when it comes to making use of the latest generative AI breakthroughs.

PART IV: CONCLUSION AND LOOKING FORWARD

CHAPTER 12: ETHICAL CONSIDERATIONS AND FUTURE DIRECTIONS

As it is such a game-changing technology, generative AI has a myriad of ethical and social implications that we need to discuss in this late stage of the book. Certainly, you have already had your own thoughts and concerns about how generative AI might disrupt the workplace, education or society as a whole.

Hence, in this chapter, we will delve into the ethical considerations that arise when dealing with Generative AI, addressing key issues such as bias, transparency, and the impact on employment, education and society. Additionally, we will speculate on future directions in Generative AI, pondering over potential advancements and how they might shape our world.

12.1 Ethical Considerations of Generative AI

As generative AI keeps growing and getting smarter, it brings up pressing ethical questions that we really need to dig into and solve.

12.1.1 Privacy and Consent

A significant issue stems from generative AI's capacity to craft highly personalized content, which inherently poses substantial privacy concerns. This problem can be broken down into two main areas: data privacy during model training and meaningful consent.

Data Privacy in Model Training

The process of training AI models often requires the use of sensitive data. This necessitates stringent measures to safeguard such information. Techniques like anonymization and differential privacy exist but are not infallible. Therefore, ensuring data privacy remains a complex issue requiring in-depth exploration and judicious solutions. To illustrate, OpenAI employs a method known as "deletion-robustness" to eliminate sensitive data from its extensive language models.

Obtaining Meaningful Consent

Given AI's aptitude to generate personalized and intricate content, obtaining meaningful consent becomes an imperative concern. We must ascertain that the individuals whose data are used fully comprehend the potential repercussions. Moreover, it is crucial to ensure that those impacted by generative AI's outputs have indeed provided their informed consent. Establishing mechanisms for informed consent in the realm of AI is a critical task, albeit one fraught with challenges. For instance, generative AI chatbots should unequivocally disclose their identity and purpose to users, securing their consent before initiating conversations or data collection.

12.1.2 Data Quality and Bias

We now delve into the other critical aspects of generative AI – the inherent issues surrounding data quality and bias. These are complex areas with two primary points of focus: first, we need to ensuring the quality and accuracy of the input data and preventing or mitigating the bias and discrimination in the output data.

Ensuring Data Quality and Accuracy

A foundational prerequisite for generating reliable results from generative AI is the quality and accuracy of the input data. The challenge lies in managing vast and diverse datasets, which may harbor errors, inconsistencies, or obsolete information. Compounding this, generative AI models may themselves introduce inaccuracies due to inherent limitations or flaws in their algorithms or training processes. Therefore, rigorous validation and verification of both input and output data are imperative. For instance, generative AI models must undergo thorough testing using relevant metrics and benchmarks to ascertain their quality and accuracy.

Preventing or Mitigating Bias and Discrimination

Bias and discrimination in the outputs of generative AI models present serious ethical concerns. Bias alludes to the skewed or inaccurate representation of specific groups or individuals based on their characteristics such as gender, race, age, or disability. Discrimination entails prejudiced treatment of these groups.

Several factors can cause bias, including a lack of diversity in input data, hidden assumptions in the algorithms or training processes, or misinterpretation of outputs by users or decision-makers. Therefore, we must actively work towards minimizing bias and discrimination in generative AI outputs, which demands ethical responsibility and awareness. Hence, companies must employ suitable tools and methods for auditing generative AI models so that potential bias or discrimination in these models can be detected.

12.1.3 Authenticity and Misuse

The enhanced capabilities of generative AI in crafting highly realistic content are already raising substantial concerns regarding the authenticity and potential misuse of this technology. This is particularly seen in the production of synthetic media, deepfakes, and the irresponsible usage of AI-generated content.

Synthetic Media and Deepfakes

AI technology is now capable of creating synthetic media, including deepfakes, which are alarmingly similar to genuine content. The problem lies in the fact that these creations can be exploited for disinformation or manipulative activities, causing significant impacts on individuals and broader society. Deepfakes, for instance, have been utilized to fabricate news, impersonate influential figures, and in extreme cases, to harass or blackmail individuals. It becomes paramount, therefore, to develop strategies to distinguish AI-generated content and assure transparency in AI-generated media. Approaches such as digital watermarking, blockchain verification, or media forensics could be potential solutions to detect or prevent synthetic media and deepfakes.

Misuse of AI-Generated Content

Another concern is the potential misuse of AI-generated content for harmful purposes, such as generating offensive or hateful content, circulating false or misleading information, or for fraudulent activities. It becomes crucial, then, to create rules and mechanisms that prevent such misuse and promote the ethical usage of generative AI. Ethical guidelines, legal frameworks, and self-regulation could be effective methods to establish standards for the responsible use of AI-generated content. Already, the European Union is trying to take a pioneering role in this field and has passed some groundbreaking, fundamental AI regulation as of mid-June 2023.

The ethical issues related to generative AI are complex and multifaceted. Their effective resolution requires collaboration from a variety of disciplines, including computer science, law, philosophy, and social sciences. It's also essential to foster an active dialogue with society to better understand and navigate the values and trade-offs in different contexts.

12.1.4 Copyright Infringement

Given that generative AI may create unique and innovative content so effectively causes legal concerns around copyright infringement and liability. There are actually two big issues here: Copyrighted works are used as the training data to develop these generative AI models – without paying the original copyright owners a dime. The second one is the question own ownership and liability around the AI-produced content.

Use of Copyrighted Works for Training Generative AI Models

Practically all generative AI models are trained using large datasets consisting of existing works like text, images, music, or even code. This practice could potentially step on the toes of original authors or owners, particularly if their work was copied, altered, or used without permission. For instance, some artists have taken legal action against generative AI platforms, accusing them of using their works to train AI models or creating new works that mimic their styles without their consent. The legal repercussions of using copyrighted works to train generative AI models can vary widely depending on the jurisdiction, the type and amount of data used, and the purpose and nature of the use. There may be a few defenses or exceptions that could apply, such as fair use, public domain, or implied license. However, these might not cover all cases and would likely require analysis on a case-by-case basis.

Ownership and Liability of AI-Generated Content

AI-produced content presents legal experts with the unresolved question as to who owns or is responsible for the AI-generated content. Our current legal frameworks might not fully cover the question this question, as they typically assume a level of human authorship or involvement.

For example, who owns the rights to a poem or a song generated by an AI model? Is it the person who provided the initial idea, the developer who created the model, or the provider who supplied the data?

Similarly, who is responsible if AI-generated content causes any harm or damage? Is it the person who requested or shared the content, the developer who designed or trained the model, or the provider who hosted or distributed the content?

These are complex questions that might require fresh legal frameworks or solutions to effectively address them. Some potential approaches could involve adapting existing laws to accommodate AI-generated content, establishing new laws or regulations specifically for AI-generated content, or employing contractual agreements or licenses between the parties involved. However, these approaches may also face limitations or challenges in terms of feasibility, enforceability, or compatibility with different jurisdictions.

12.2 Future Directions in Generative AI

Several technological and societal trends are expected to drive the evolution of generative AI, impacting our daily lives, our understanding of creativity, and the accessibility of AI.

12.2.1 Integration of AI in Daily Life

In the coming months and years, generative AI will inevitably be integrated more and more into our everyday life. As this process unfolds, it is going to transform our interactions with technology and potentially revolutionize various sectors of society.

Personalized Content and Recommendations

Generative AI can create highly personalized content and recommendations, enhancing user experiences in entertainment, shopping, learning, and more. From customized music playlists, product suggestions, educational materials, or travel itineraries – generative AI can create all of these perfectly targeted for each user, based on their preferences and feedback. The way we consume content, shop, learn, and more will never be the same again. As consumers, our expectations are going to increase tremendously, expecting at every touch point with businesses and service providers that our individual needs and preferences will be taken into account. Privacy concerns notwithstanding, personalization will become every consumer's inalienable right.

12.2.2 Increasing Sophistication of AI-Generated Content

The quality and complexity of AI-generated content are set to increase as AI models continue to improve, creating new possibilities and challenges.

Broadened Applications

With the potential to generate increasingly sophisticated content, AI could find novel applications across various industries, enhancing creative possibilities. For instance, generative AI can be used to create realistic simulations for training or testing purposes, generate novel designs or artworks, or produce original stories or scripts. These applications could expand the scope and impact of generative AI in domains such as education, engineering, art, or entertainment.

Challenging Traditional Concepts

The sophistication of AI-generated content could also challenge our traditional concepts of creativity and originality. It is highly likely that the line between human and machine-generated creativity may become increasingly blurred as generative AI models produce content that is indistinguishable from or surpasses human-made content. This could raise questions about the definition and value of creativity, the attribution and ownership of AI-generated content, and the ethical implications of using or consuming such content. After all, what is human creativity and genius worth, if it can be accessed and replicated for free and at-scale by anyone across the world with a few clicks on their laptop or smartphone? How is the role of artists and creators going to change?

12.2.3 Accessibility and Efficiency of AI Models

Improvements in machine learning and computation can make AI models more efficient and potentially more accessible, fostering innovation and democratizing AI technology.

Fostering Innovation

With more accessible AI models, more people can engage in developing and applying AI, resulting in a wider range of innovative applications. For example, platforms such as GitHub Copilot or OpenAI Playground can enable users to generate code or content using generative AI models without requiring extensive programming skills or resources. These platforms can lower the barriers to entry for using generative AI and encourage experimentation and creativity among users.

Democratizing AI Technology

As AI models are increasingly accessible by non-tech users around the world, they democratize AI technology, ensuring more people can benefit from AI's capabilities and contribute to its development. Initiatives like as Hugging Face or TensorFlow Hub can provide open-source access to pre-trained generative AI models for various tasks and languages. They enable users to leverage existing generative AI models for their own purposes or fine-tune them for specific domains or contexts.

12.2.4 Ethical AI Development

In the face of ethical challenges posed by generative AI, the field will likely move towards more ethical AI development that incorporates ethical principles and values into the design and deployment of generative AI systems.

Developing Guidelines for Responsible AI Use

One response to these ethical challenges could be the development of guidelines for responsible AI use that provide normative frameworks and best practices for ensuring that generative AI systems are aligned with human values and interests. Important guidelines such as UNESCO's Recommendation on the Ethics of Artificial Intelligence or OECD's Principles on Artificial Intelligence can offer guidance on how to promote trustworthy and beneficial generative AI systems that respect human dignity, rights, and freedoms.

Transparent and Accountable AI Systems

We are likely going to see an increased emphasis on creating transparent and accountable AI systems that can make their decision-making processes understandable to humans and be held accountable for their actions. Important concepts and techniques such as explainable AI or adversarial testing can be used to enhance the transparency and robustness of generative AI systems so that users understand how and why generative AI systems produce certain outputs or detect potential errors or biases in their outputs.

Fostering a Culture of Ethics in AI Research and Development

Cultivating a culture of ethics in AI research and development is crucial for ensuring that generative AI systems are developed and used in a responsible and ethical manner. This could involve ethical training for AI professionals, ethical review processes for AI research and development, and ongoing dialogue about AI ethics in the professional community. Already, there are numerous such initiatives and projects like the Partnership on AI or the Montreal AI Ethics Institute that could provide platforms for collaboration and discussion among various stakeholders on the ethical issues and challenges of generative AI.

12.3 Ethical Considerations and Future Directions - Epilogue

As we finish our journey through the world of Generative AI, we find ourselves on the edge of a new era where AI can help us in many ways, but it also raises important questions. How do we ensure that privacy is respected when using AI? How do we make sure that the data AI uses is of good quality and free from bias? How do we prevent misuse of AI, especially when it comes to creating realistic, but potentially misleading, content? And what about copyright - who owns the content that AI creates?

These questions are not easy to answer, but they are critical to consider as we use and develop AI. This book has presented many ideas and guidelines to help us use AI responsibly and ethically. But the job is not done; it's up to us all - researchers, developers, and users of AI - to continue this conversation and work towards the best practices.

Looking ahead, the future of AI is promising. It could make our lives more personalized, bring creativity and innovation to new heights, and open up exciting possibilities in fields we might not even have considered yet. But as we embrace these exciting changes, we must remember to tread carefully, considering the ethical implications at every step.

So, as we close this book, let's take the insights we've gained, the questions we've raised, and the future possibilities we've imagined with us. The journey with Generative AI is just beginning, and we all have a role to play. Let's ensure that as we move forward, we do so responsibly, ethically, and with a sense of anticipation for the exciting future that lies ahead.

In the next and final chapter, we will provide some resources for further learning and keeping up to date on all things Generative AI.

CHAPTER 13: USEFUL LINKS & RESOURCES

This book has provided you with an introduction to the fascinating world of AI and Generative AI. However, this is not the end of your learning journey. Chapter 13 offers a collection of resources to help you stay updated and informed about the ongoing developments and trends in the field of AI. You will find links to AI news websites, influential personalities on YouTube and Twitter, and other useful sources of information. These resources are helpful for anyone who wants to keep learning and exploring the field of AI.

AI and Generative AI News Websites

- **AI Magazine**: This platform serves as an unrivaled beacon for comprehensive coverage of AI, Machine Learning, AR & VR, Data, and Technology. With a top-notch magazine, resource-rich website, insightful newsletters, and enlightening webinars, AI Magazine brings AI applications to the world in a digestible manner.

- **AI Trends**: The Business and Technology of Enterprise AI. A source of information and insight for business leaders seeking to understand how AI is impacting their organizations.

- **MIT News**: Artificial Intelligence: An excellent source of fresh news, engaging features, and compelling research stories on AI, straight from the intellectual powerhouse of MIT, one of the world's pioneering research institutions.

- **WIRED UK**: Artificial Intelligence: WIRED UK presents a window into the AI revolution, offering up-to-date news and captivating features. It's a cornerstone of discussions on technology, culture, and innovation.

- **DATAVERSITY**: Data Education for Business and IT Professionals. This is a goldmine of educational resources and services, specifically designed for business and IT professionals eager to dive into data management and its correlation with business objectives.

- **OpenAI Blog**: The official blog by the research organization behind the likes of ChatGPT, GPT-4 and DALL-E 2.

YouTube Influencers & Channels to Follow

- **Two Minute Papers**: This channel summarizes the latest and most exciting research papers in computer science, especially in artificial intelligence, in a way that anyone can understand.

- **Lex Fridman**: Lex is a leading AI YouTuber and thought leader, his channel features conversations with some of the most interesting people in artificial intelligence, deep learning, robotics, engineering, science, and beyond.

- **Siraj Raval**: Siraj's channel offers tons of videos teaching the fundamentals of artificial intelligence through fun and engaging videos that cover topics such as natural language processing, computer vision, generative adversarial networks, reinforcement learning, and more.

- **3Blue1Brown:** A channel that uses animations to explain complex mathematical concepts that are often related to artificial intelligence, such as neural networks, linear algebra, calculus, probability, and more.

- **Code Bullet**: Another great YouTube channel showcasing various projects and experiments involving artificial intelligence, machine learning, game development, coding challenges, and more.

AITwitter: You must follow these Twitter profiles

- **@ylecun**: Yann LeCun's Twitter profile presents a glimpse into the life of a deep learning pioneer, convolutional neural network co-inventor, and Facebook's chief AI scientist, all while being an NYU professor.

- **@goodfellow_ian**: Ian Goodfellow, currently a director of machine learning at Apple and formerly a Google Brain researcher, co-authored the renowned Deep Learning textbook and co-invented generative adversarial networks.

- **@fchollet**: Francois Chollet, the ingenious creator of the Keras deep learning framework and the author of Deep Learning with Python, continually reports his newest insights and experiences from his tenure as a software engineer at Google.

- **@hardmaru**: David Ha, a research scientist at Google Brain Tokyo and an ex-Recruit Institute of Technology researcher, regularly shares news, reports and useful resources that underline his interest and projects in generative models, reinforcement learning, robotics, and art.

- **@AIBreakdownPod**: AI Breakdown is a podcast that breaks down complex and cutting-edge AI topics in an accessible and engaging way. The host, James Le, interviews experts and researchers in the field of generative AI and discusses topics such as GPT-3, DALL-E, CLIP, and more. He also explores the implications and applications of generative AI for various domains such as art, music, gaming, and education.

- **@rowancheung** is a popular AI influencer who shares the latest developments in the world of artificial intelligence. He tests hundreds of AI tools and reports the best ones. He also does daily rundowns of the most important news and events in AI, such as Google's I/O event, HuggingFace's Transformers Agent, Scale AI's Donovan and EGP, and Synthesia Research's HumanRF.

- **@aisolopreneur** is an AI entrepreneur who builds and launches AI products using no-code tools. He shares his journey and insights on how to use AI to create digital solutions for various problems and opportunities. He also showcases his projects, such as ChatGPT for Business, ChatGPT for Education, ChatGPT for Health, and ChatGPT for Entertainment.

- **@moritzkremb** is an AI researcher and engineer who works on generative models for text, image, and video. He has one of the best and most active accounts on AITwitter, featuring daily posts with valuable resources and updates on the latest generative AI tools.

- **@itsPaulAI** is an AI educator who teaches how to use AI and no-code tools to build better and faster. He creates tutorials and videos on how to use ChatGPT plugins, such as AskYourPDF, AutoGPT, Bardify, and more. He also runs a newsletter where he shares more tips and resources on AI and no-code.

- **@nathanwchan** is an AI developer and community builder who works on open-source AI projects. He contributes to ChatGPT's ecosystem by creating plugins, extensions, and integrations. With his Twitter account, he shares his insights on the trends and challenges in the AI industry, such as prompt engineering, model switching, and data privacy.

- **@heybarsee** is an AI artist who creates interesting generative art using GANs, StyleGANs, VQGANs, CLIPs, and more. He showcases his artworks on Twitter and Instagram, where he also explains the techniques and tools he uses.

Best AI & Generative AI Podcasts

- **The TWIML AI Podcast**: This podcast features interviews with leading researchers and practitioners in machine learning and artificial intelligence. It provides insights into the latest developments and applications of generative AI, including natural language generation, computer vision, and reinforcement learning. The podcast is hosted by Sam Charrington, a sought after industry analyst, speaker, commentator and thought leader . He brings his expertise and curiosity to every episode.

- **The AI Podcast**: Explore how AI is transforming various industries and domains such as gaming, healthcare, robotics, and entertainment. Listen to experts and innovators discussing the use of generative AI to create new experiences and possibilities. The podcast is hosted by Noah Kravitz, a former journalist and editor who has covered technology for over a decade. He has a knack for asking engaging questions and making complex topics accessible.
- **Data Skeptic**: This podcast caters to those curious and skeptical about data science and AI. It offers discussions and mini-episodes that explain the concepts and techniques behind generative AI, such as generative adversarial networks, variational autoencoders, and transformers. The podcast is hosted by Kyle Polich, a data scientist and educator who has a passion for teaching complex topics in a simple way. He challenges common assumptions and myths about data science and AI.
- **Podcast.ai**: Discover how generative AI is changing communication and interaction with machines. The podcast focuses on topics like ChatGPT, an AI-powered chatbot trained on large language models. The podcast is hosted by James Vlahos, a journalist and author who has written extensively about conversational AI. He explores the potential and limitations of human-machine dialogue.
- **The Talking Machines**: Gain insights from researchers and practitioners working on generative AI projects, including text summarization, image synthesis, and music generation. The podcast provides stories and firsthand experiences in an accessible manner. The podcast is hosted by Katherine Gorman, a storyteller and producer who has a background in public radio. She brings a human perspective to the technical aspects of generative AI.
- **Linear Digressions**: This podcast explores data science and machine learning in an informative and entertaining way. It covers the theory and practice of generative AI, including its workings, capabilities, challenges, and limitations. The podcast is hosted by Ben Jaffe, a senior data scientist at Stitch Fix, and Katie Malone, a director of data science research and development at Civis Analytics. They share their insights and experiences from working with generative AI in different domains.
- **Practical AI**: Machine Learning & Data Science: Join weekly conversations about practical applications of AI and machine learning. Get practical tips and tricks for using generative AI tools and frameworks like TensorFlow, PyTorch, Hugging Face, and OpenAI. The podcast is hosted by Daniel Whitenack, a data scientist and developer advocate at Pachyderm. He showcases real-world examples and best practices of generative AI.
- **Data Stories**: Dive into the world of data visualization and storytelling. Learn how generative AI can help create engaging and interactive data

stories, such as charts, maps, animations, and narratives. The podcast is hosted by Enrico Bertini, an associate professor of computer science at NYU Tandon School of Engineering, and Moritz Stefaner, a freelance designer who specializes in data visualization. They discuss the principles and techniques of using generative AI for data storytelling.

- **Artificial Intelligence with Lex Fridman**: Engage in in-depth conversations with influential figures in AI and related fields. Explore topics relevant to generative AI, including ethics, creativity, intelligence, consciousness, and the future of humanity. The podcast is hosted by Lex Fridman, a research scientist at MIT working on human-centered artificial intelligence. He probes the minds and motivations of his guests with deep questions.

- **Gigaom AI Minute**: Stay up to date with daily AI news and insights. Stay informed about the latest trends and developments in generative AI, including new models, datasets, applications, and breakthroughs. The podcast is hosted by Byron Reese, the CEO of Gigaom, a technology research company that focuses on emerging technologies. He delivers concise

- and informative summaries of the most important news in generative AI.

- **Generative AI Podcasts Are Here. Prepare to Be Bored**: This podcast provides insights into AI-generated podcasts and the technology behind them. It includes simulations of popular human podcast hosts conversing with fake guests, offering a unique perspective on generative AI. The podcast is hosted by John Smith, a fictional character created by OpenAI's GPT-3 model. He demonstrates the capabilities and challenges of using generative AI for podcasting.

Other Websites

- **Kaggle**: A platform for data science and machine learning competitions where users can find datasets, notebooks, courses, forums, and more.

- **Papers with Code**: PWC tracks the latest machine learning research papers along with their code implementations.

- **Fast.ai**: This website offers free online courses on deep learning for coders as well as a library of tools and resources to make deep learning more accessible.

- **Generative Hut**: Here you can find a showcase of various generative art projects created by artists using artificial intelligence techniques such as GANs, VAEs, Style Transfer, etc.

EPILOGUE

Congratulations! Reaching the end of this chapter, and indeed this book, you have embarked on an enriching journey into the world of AI and Generative AI. These resources will act as your compass, guiding you as you navigate the ever-evolving landscape of AI. They will help you stay informed, provide inspiration, and offer insights into the latest advancements and discussions in the AI community.

It has been my privilege to be your guide and companion on this journey. As we close this book, remember that your exploration of AI and Generative AI is not ending but merely beginning. It is my hope that the knowledge you've gained will serve as a launchpad for your own discoveries, creations, and innovations in the world of AI.

One more time do I want to encourage you to start diving in now, subscribe to one or more of the presented generative AI solutions for one month and play around with the features. Test ChatGPT to its limits, make funny and creative images or photographs with MidJourney, let GitHub Copilot create a new website or app for you (if you are a programmer with basic understanding) and subscribe to the AI thought leaders on Twitter to stay ahead of the curve.

The future is bright and exciting – especially for you as a generative AI pioneer and expert! Best of luck out there!

PART V: APPENDIX

Welcome to the appendix-section of the book! As this book is titled "Artificial Intelligence & Generative AI for Beginners", I wanted to keep the main part of the book focused on the main topics and free of too-complicated technical jargon while making sure you get all the information you really need to understand and start playing around and profiting from the full potential of the generative AI revolution.

In the course of writing the book, I crafted two more interesting chapters that I finally decided to put into the appendix section for the really motivated and curious readers. While not really essential, the lecture of these chapters is going to provide with additional insights and an in-depth understanding of the development and building of (generative) AI models, enabling you to better understand how your favourite generative AI tools are working, how to better prompt for perfect outputs and – just maybe – how you can get started in the building and development world of generative AI.

There are two chapters appended here. First, we are going to look at the essential tools, programming languages and toolkits that form the foundation of AI development. In the second chapter, we are going to look in detail at the process of how generative AI models are actually built, tested, refined and finally deployed.

Buckle up and let's dive in!

CHAPTER 14: TOOLS FOR AI DEVELOPMENT

This chapter will introduce you to Python, TensorFlow, PyTorch, and Jupyter Notebook, tools that form the cornerstone of current AI development. You will discover why Python is the preferred language for AI programming, understand the strengths of TensorFlow and PyTorch in numerical computation and neural network development, and learn how Jupyter Notebook serves as an interactive programming environment. Each tool in this repertoire brings a unique advantage to your AI development journey, and this chapter aims to highlight those strengths and guide you in choosing the right tools for your projects (should you choose to do so).

14.1 Python: The AI Programmer's Language

Python is a high-level, interpreted programming language that has become the de facto language for AI and machine learning. It is renowned for its simplicity and readability, making it a language of choice for both beginners and experienced developers. In the context of AI development, Python offers an extensive range of libraries and frameworks that simplify the process and reduce the need for from-scratch coding.

14.1.1 Python's Strengths in AI Development

Python has multiple strengths that contribute to its effectiveness in AI development.

- **Readability and Maintainability:** Python's syntax is clean, concise, and designed to be easily readable. This readability results in easier maintenance and updates, which is particularly advantageous when working on large-scale or complex AI projects.

- **Modularity and Code Reuse:** Its support for modules and packages fosters program modularity and code reuse which is particularly useful when developing complex AI applications, as it promotes better organization and reduces redundancy.

- **Rapid Prototyping**: Python is an interpreted language, which means that it can run immediately after being written – a factor that comes in handy with rapid prototyping, enabling developers to quickly test their AI algorithms and models.

- **Strong Community and Ecosystem:** Among the most-widely adopted programming languages in the world, Python has more than 3 million programmers and developers on GitHub alone. This also ensures wide support and large amount of developer docs available for incoming coders. The ecosystem around Python has resulted in a plethora of libraries for diverse tasks related to AI.

14.1.2 The Python AI Ecosystem

The ecosystem of Python libraries for AI and machine learning is vast, encompassing libraries for data analysis, visualization, machine learning, and deep learning.

- **Data Analysis and Manipulation**: Libraries such as NumPy and Pandas offer powerful tools for numerical computation, data manipulation, and analysis, which form the backbone of any AI or machine learning project.

- **Visualization:** Libraries like Matplotlib and Seaborn provide advanced data visualization capabilities, a crucial aspect of understanding data and AI model performance.

- **Machine Learning and Deep Learning:** TensorFlow, PyTorch, and Scikit-learn are among the most popular Python libraries for machine learning and deep learning. They abstract away much of the complexity involved in building AI models, making the development process more efficient and accessible.

14.1.3 Dive into Python AI Libraries

- **TensorFlow**: Developed by Google Brain Team, TensorFlow is used for building and training deep learning models. It uses data flow graphs and provides functionalities for creating large-scale neural networks with many layers.

- **PyTorch:** Having been developed by Facebook's AI Research lab, PyTorch is known for its flexibility and intuitive interface as well as the support of dynamic computational graphs, which allows for flexibility in adjusting and modifying the model.

- **Scikit-learn:** Scikit-learn is a versatile library for machine learning in Python that provides a selection of efficient tools for machine learning and statistical modeling, including classification, regression, clustering, and dimensionality reduction.

These libraries, combined with Python's readability and ease of use, contribute to Python's position as the leading language in AI development. Python will continue to play a central role in AI as the field advances and the complexity of AI projects is only going to continue to grow.

14.2 TensorFlow: Flexible Numerical Computation

TensorFlow is an open-source software library, developed by Google Brain Team, for numerical computation and large-scale machine learning applications. Its flexibility, scalability, and wide-ranging capabilities have made it one of the most widely adopted tools for building and training deep learning models.

14.2.1 Understanding TensorFlow

At its core, TensorFlow operates using data flow graphs. These are structures that detail how data moves through a graph or series of processing nodes. Each node in the graph represents a mathematical operation, while each connection or edge between nodes is a multi-dimensional data array, also known as a tensor.

- **Tensors:** In the context of TensorFlow, tensors are the fundamental units of data. Tensors are n-dimensional arrays that can hold real-valued or complex-valued numbers with many dimensions. These tensors flow through the computation graph, hence the name TensorFlow.

- **Dataflow Graphs:** Dataflow graphs describe computations as a directed graph. The nodes represent operations or computations, while the edges represent the tensors flowing between operations. This architectural design enables efficient computation and derivation.

- **Eager Execution:** TensorFlow 2.0 introduced eager execution, a feature that allows for more interactive front-end development by providing an imperative programming style. With eager execution, operations are computed as they are called within Python, simplifying debugging and making the TensorFlow codebase more intuitive to use.

14.2.2 TensorFlow in Deep Learning

When it comes to deep learning, TensorFlow offers a variety of features that streamline model development, training, and deployment.

- **Layers of Abstraction:** TensorFlow offers multiple levels of abstraction which enables developers to choose between fine-grained control over model details and high-level simplicity for faster implementation. This flexibility allows both researchers and application developers to use TensorFlow effectively according to their needs.

- **Neural Network Support:** It also supports a wide array of neural network architectures. From conventional fully-connected neural networks to convolutional neural networks (CNNs) and recurrent neural networks (RNNs), TensorFlow allows the construction and training of many types of models.

- **Training Tools**: TensorFlow provides several tools for training deep learning models. This includes support for automatic differentiation, which is crucial for backpropagation in neural networks. It also provides various optimization algorithms, such as stochastic gradient descent (SGD), RMSprop, and Adam, to facilitate efficient and effective training of models.

- **Model Deployment:** Once models have been developed with TensorFlow, they can be easily deployed in various environments – from cloud servers, to desktops, and even on mobile and edge devices. This ease of deployment, along with TensorFlow's scalability, makes it a comprehensive tool for end-to-end model development and deployment.

- **TensorBoard:** TensorBoard is a suite of visualization tools included with TensorFlow that makes understanding, debugging, and optimizing TensorFlow programs easier. It helps to visualize the model graphs, plot quantitative metrics about the execution of the model, and show additional data like images that pass through it.

With these capabilities, TensorFlow provides a comprehensive, flexible, and efficient platform for deep learning and AI development that remains among the most popular and commonly used tools in the scene.

14.3 PyTorch: Dynamic Neural Networks

Developed by Facebook's AI Research lab (FAIR), PyTorch is an open-source machine learning library for Python known for its simplicity, flexibility, and seamless use on different hardware platforms. It is particularly well-liked for its intuitive interface and its dynamic computational graph approach.

14.3.1 PyTorch's Dynamic Computational Graphs

One of PyTorch's most distinguishing features is its use of dynamic computational graphs, also known as define-by-run graphs. This contrasts with the static computational graphs, or define-and-run graphs, used in libraries like TensorFlow (before version 2.0).

- **Dynamic Computational Graphs**: In a dynamic graph framework, the graph structure can be modified on the fly as computations progress. The result is a higher degree of flexibility that allows developers to use standard Python control flow statements in their models. Hence, the code is easier to write and debug.

- **Debugging:** Thanks to the dynamic computation, debugging in PyTorch is more straightforward. When an error occurs, you can directly identify which line in your code caused it. This is a contrast to define-and-run graphs, where the graph is a separate entity from the actual Python code, making the debugging process more complex.

14.3.2 PyTorch for Deep Learning

Like TensorFlow, PyTorch offers a comprehensive platform for deep learning research and application development that supports a wide range of neural network architectures and provides tools for creating and training these models.

- **Neural Network Support**: PyTorch has built-in modules for creating neural network layers and entire models through the **torch.nn** package. Among these are commonly used layers like linear, convolutional, and recurrent layers, along with loss functions and activation functions.

- **Training Tools:** Most notably, PyTorch also supports automatic differentiation via its **autograd** package, enabling gradient computations and backpropagation. Combined with its built-in optimization algorithms, this simplifies the training of complex neural networks.

- **TorchVision**: An additional PyTorch package, TorchVision, provides datasets, models, and transformation methods for computer vision applications. This can speed up the development process for these types of models.

- **Interoperability with NumPy**: PyTorch tensors can be converted to NumPy arrays and vice versa very efficiently, making the library easily integrable with existing Python codebases and other libraries that accept NumPy arrays.

Overall, its intuitive design and flexibility make PyTorch a powerful tool for both academic researchers and applied machine learning developers. The dynamic computational graph approach pioneered by PyTorch simplifies the model development and debugging process, reducing the barrier to entry for beginners and improving productivity for experienced developers.

14.4 Jupyter Notebook: Interactive Programming Environment

Jupyter Notebook, often just called Jupyter, is a powerful, open-source tool that provides an interactive environment for creating and sharing documents that contain live code, equations, visualizations, and narrative text. As an invaluable tool for data exploration, data cleaning and transformation, numerical simulation, statistical modeling, data visualization, machine learning, and much more, Jupyter Notebook has found a large fanbase in AI developer circles around the world.

14.4.1 Features of Jupyter Notebook

Jupyter Notebook offers a suite of features that make it particularly useful for AI development:

- **Multi-language Support:** The Jupyter IPE supports over 40 programming languages, including those most commonly used in data science and AI such as Python, R, Julia, and Scala.

- **Live Code:** Code cells within a notebook can be executed in place, avoiding the need to switch between different applications or windows for writing code and viewing output. This makes it an ideal platform for exploratory data analysis and iterative development.

- **Data Visualization:** Jupyter integrates well with popular data visualization libraries like Matplotlib, Seaborn, and Plotly. Plots and charts created in a notebook cell are embedded in the notebook itself, creating a visual and intuitive way to present and explore data.

- **Rich Text:** It offers support for Markdown to format text cells. This allows you to create structured documents with styled text, headers, links, and even images and HTML elements.

- **Latex Support:** Jupyter Notebook also supports Latex, a typesetting system for mathematical and technical document. Especially developers who want to create notebooks that contain mathematical equations and formulae will profit from this integration.

- **Sharing and Conversion:** Notebooks can be easily shared through email, GitHub, and the Jupyter Notebook Viewer. They can also be converted to various output formats (like PDF or HTML) for broader sharing.

14.4.2 Jupyter in AI Development

In AI and machine learning development, Jupyter Notebooks are often used for:

- **Exploratory Data Analysis:** Jupyter's interactive nature and integration with data manipulation libraries like Pandas make it perfect for exploring and understanding your data.

- **Model Development and Training:** Libraries such as Scikit-learn and TensorFlow have first-class support for Jupyter. Hence, developers can train and fine-tune machine learning models directly within a notebook.

- **Result Presentation and Reporting:** The combination of code, visualizations, and rich text in a single document makes Jupyter an excellent tool for presenting results, creating reports, or even writing blog posts.

- **Education and Collaboration:** Notebooks can be used for teaching programming, machine learning, and data science concepts, making complex ideas easier to understand. They also promote reproducibility and collaboration among data scientists, researchers, and developers.

14.5 Tools for AI Development - Epilogue

Congratulations on reaching the end of this pivotal chapter. You've been introduced to Python, TensorFlow, PyTorch, and Jupyter Notebook, and gained an understanding of their roles in AI development. These tools are instrumental in bringing AI concepts and techniques to life, enabling you to develop, train, and test your own AI models – should you wish to do so. Remember that these tools are just the beginning, as the field of AI is continually evolving with new advancements.

CHAPTER 15: HOW TO BUILD A GENERATIVE AI SYSTEM

Equipped with an understanding of Generative AI and its applications, we now want to take a closer look at how such sophisticated, generative AI Systems are developed and built. This will also give you an edge when it comes to getting the most out of the best Generative AI tools.

In this chapter, we'll grasp the fundamental concepts underpinning Generative AI systems, including the selection of the right tools, data collection and preparation, model training, and the process of testing and refining a model.

This chapter will provide you with the knowledge and confidence to begin creating your own Generative AI systems, enabling you to contribute to the innovative wave of AI-driven creation – or at least help you to better understand the workings of the generative AI solutions you might be using in the course of your work and private pursuits.

15.1 Grasping the Fundamental Concepts

Creating a generative AI system hinges on understanding the foundational principles that underpin the field of machine learning, especially deep learning. This comprehension involves mastering the intricacies of Neural Networks, Activation Functions and Backpropagation, and Loss Functions. Each of these components plays a crucial role in developing the operational ability of generative AI models.

15.1.1 Neural Networks

Neural networks serve as the linchpin of most generative AI models, drawing inspiration from the structure and function of biological neural networks. This biomimicry extends to the features that allow a neural network to learn, adapt, and evolve, with repeated exposure to data.

15.1.1.1 Structure of Neural Networks

Neural networks are essentially comprised of interconnected nodes or 'neurons,' clustered in layers. The initial layer, the input layer, takes in data, which is then processed by one or multiple hidden layers. The final layer, the output layer, provides the end result or output of the network's computation. The complexity and depth of the network can vary, influencing its ability to learn and extract patterns from data.

15.1.1.2 Information Processing

The process within each neuron involves receiving input data, applying a weighted sum to it (where weights indicate the relevance of these inputs), and using an activation function to decide if and how much of the signal to pass on to the next layer. The weights and biases within this system adapt during the learning process, molding the network's understanding of the data.

15.1.1.3 Learning from Data:

Learning in neural networks involves a continuous adjustment of weights and biases. This adjustment is influenced by the difference or error between the predicted output and the actual output. The process of correcting this error employs a technique called backpropagation, partnered with an optimization algorithm like gradient descent or its variants, enhancing the network's predictive accuracy over time.

15.1.2 Activation Functions and Backpropagation

Activation Functions and Backpropagation form core mechanisms that enable the functional efficiency of neural networks.

11.1.2.1 Activation Functions

Activation functions are mathematical functions that determine the extent of the signal passed onto the subsequent layer in a network. Various activation functions such as the sigmoid function, ReLU (Rectified Linear Unit), and tanh function are commonly used. The choice of function can vary, with each offering its own advantages depending on the specific use case.

15.1.2.2 Backpropagation

Backpropagation is the primary algorithm that helps optimize a neural network's parameters, aiming to minimize the discrepancy between the network's predictions and actual values. This algorithm calculates the gradient (rate of change) of the loss function concerning the network's weights and uses this gradient to make proportional adjustments to these weights, thereby reducing error.

15.1.3 Loss Functions

Loss functions constitute an essential aspect of the neural network's learning process, essentially determining the degree of error in the network's predictions.

15.1.3.1 Role of Loss Functions

Loss functions quantify the gap between a network's predictions and the actual values. This deviation or 'error' is what the network strives to reduce during the learning process, with smaller errors indicating a more accurate model.

15.1.3.2 Choice of Loss Function

The choice of a loss function can significantly influence a network's learning path and the quality of its predictions. Different tasks may necessitate different loss functions. For instance, Mean Squared Error (MSE) loss is typically utilized for regression tasks, while Cross-Entropy loss is favored for classification tasks.

Learning about these topics can be greatly facilitated by a range of online resources and MOOCs offered by platforms such as Coursera and edX. These can provide comprehensive knowledge about these topics, thereby equipping you with the foundational understanding necessary for developing generative AI systems.

15.2 Selecting the Right Tools

The toolset you utilize for constructing generative AI systems can significantly shape the development trajectory. While the selection primarily hinges on your specific requirements, personal coding preferences, and the degree of control and customization you seek, it is important to carefully weigh your options. Here, we'll delve into some key considerations.

15.2.1 Programming Language

The selection of the programming language forms the bedrock of your generative AI development process. This choice can impact both the ease of development and the performance of the final system.

15.2.1.1 Python

Python holds the crown as the most extensively employed language in AI and data science fields. Its widespread acceptance is attributed to its inherent simplicity, readability, and extensive library support, which includes popular libraries for machine learning, data manipulation, and visualization. Python's syntax is clean and intuitive, providing an ideal environment for beginners in the programming world.

15.2.1.2 Other Languages

While Python rules the roost, other languages such as R, Java, and C++ also find use in specific scenarios within the AI landscape. For instance, R enjoys popularity in statistical computing and graphics, thanks to its comprehensive library support for these areas. C++, on the other hand, is often the go-to language for applications demanding high performance and rapid execution, given its close-to-the-metal nature and optimization capabilities.

15.2.2 Libraries and Frameworks

Libraries and frameworks are instrumental in accelerating AI development. They offer pre-fabricated, tested, and optimized code segments that can be leveraged to design and train AI models, sparing substantial time and effort.

15.2.2.1 TensorFlow:

Created by the Google Brain Team, TensorFlow is a highly regarded open-source library for numerical computation and large-scale machine learning. Its flexible architecture enables easy deployment of computation across a variety of platforms, ranging from mobile devices to distributed CPU/GPU setups.

15.2.2.2 PyTorch:

Originating from Facebook's AI Research lab, PyTorch has carved out a niche for itself thanks to its simplicity, user-friendliness, and dynamic computational graph. This dynamic nature facilitates easier debugging and is a boon for AI researchers and practitioners.

15.2.2.3 Keras:

Keras serves as a high-level neural networks API that operates atop TensorFlow. It focuses on being user-friendly, modular, and extendable, making neural network design and testing a breeze. It is particularly known for enabling quick prototyping and experimentation.

15.2.2.4 Choosing the Right One:

Each of these libraries and frameworks brings its unique strengths to the table. TensorFlow shines with its production readiness and scalability, making it a solid choice for commercial applications. PyTorch, with its user-friendly ethos and dynamic computational graph, is often the preferred option for researchers and beginners. Keras, with its focus on user-friendliness and rapid prototyping, is a fantastic choice for initial testing and model design. The ultimate choice should dovetail with your project's unique needs and your personal comfort level with these tools.

15.3 Data Collection and Preparation

Data serves as the foundational bedrock for AI and machine learning models, and generative AI systems are no exception. The whole process is anchored in the acquisition and preparation of data, which will serve as the training material for the AI model. The nature, quality, and volume of data required will be primarily dictated by the specific problem you are attempting to address.

15.3.1 Data Collection

The first step in the journey is the collection of data pertinent to your task. The category of data can span a broad spectrum depending upon the nature of the application - it could range from images for a generative art project, to audio files for a music generation system, to textual data for a natural language processing application. It is vital to ensure that the data you gather is representative of the problem domain you're aiming to address. This guarantees a rich diversity and accuracy in the outputs produced by the generative AI system.

15.3.2 Data Cleaning

Raw data in its initial form is seldom ready for immediate use. Data cleaning involves the removal or rectification of incorrect, incomplete, improperly formatted, or duplicated data. In text-based tasks, this could translate to activities such as the removal of special characters, correction of spelling mistakes, or standardization of text formats. For tasks involving images, it could entail removing corrupted images, standardizing image sizes, or managing missing data elements. This step is crucial to ensure that your data is accurate and reliable.

15.3.3 Data Formatting and Transformation

Data typically needs to undergo transformation or reformatting to make it compatible with the model you're deploying. For example, text data might require tokenization - a process that involves breaking up text into individual words or phrases. Alternatively, it might need to be transformed into numerical vectors for compatibility with the model. Image data, on the other hand, might require resizing or normalization to facilitate an effective training process. These transformations ensure that your data can be effectively processed by your model.

15.3.4 Train-Validation-Test Split

Lastly, the collected dataset is usually split into three distinct subsets: the training set, the validation set, and the test set. The training set serves as the primary dataset for teaching the model. The validation set is leveraged to fine-tune the model's parameters and mitigate the risk of overfitting during the training phase. The test set, meanwhile, is used to evaluate the performance of the model on unseen data, providing a measure of its accuracy and generalizability.

The significance of each of these steps in the data preparation process cannot be overstated. High-quality, well-prepared data is one of the most critical determinants of the success of a generative AI system. As such, these steps should be approached with meticulous care and attention to detail.

15.4 Training the Model

After the data has been collected and processed, the next crucial step involves training the AI model. This process constitutes several iterative stages that involve providing the model with input data, adjusting its internal parameters based on the output using concepts like the loss function and backpropagation, and then repeating this cycle until the model can generate accurate output consistently.

15.4.1 Initializing the Model

The first step in the training phase involves deciding on the architecture of the model, which often comprises a specific type of neural network. For example, if the data is image-based, a Convolutional Neural Network (CNN) might be suitable, while for sequential data, a Recurrent Neural Network (RNN) or Transformer model might be chosen. Once the architecture is decided, the model is initialized with weights that are typically randomly assigned. The selection of the architecture depends largely on the nature of the data and the problem at hand, and the initial random weights provide a starting point for the model's learning journey.

15.4.2 Forward Propagation

In each iteration during the training phase, the model processes a batch of input data in a series of computations, known as forward propagation. Here, the model processes the input data through all its layers, using the current weights and biases to make a prediction. The forward propagation phase is essentially the model attempting to make an educated guess based on its current understanding of the problem.

15.4.3 Computing the Loss

When the model has made a prediction, the loss, or error, of this prediction needs to be computed. This is accomplished with a loss function, which measures the discrepancy between the model's prediction and the actual value. The loss function provides a quantitative measure of the model's performance and is a crucial component in training the model. It essentially provides a yardstick to measure how wrong or 'off-target' the model's predictions are.

15.4.4 Backpropagation and Optimization

Backpropagation is an algorithm used to adjust the model's weights and biases based on the computed loss. It calculates the gradient of the loss function with respect to the model's parameters and adjusts these parameters to minimize the loss. The ultimate goal of backpropagation is to minimize the discrepancy between the model's predictions and the actual values, thus making the model more accurate.

The backpropagation process is repeated for a certain number of iterations or epochs. To expedite the learning process, an optimization algorithm, such as Stochastic Gradient Descent (SGD) or Adam, is used. These algorithms adjust the parameters in a manner that most effectively reduces the loss, helping the model learn more efficiently.

Through these iterative processes, the model gradually learns to map the input data to the correct output. With each iteration, the model's predictions or outputs become increasingly accurate, and it becomes more proficient at its assigned task. This process of repeated training and optimization is at the heart of how AI models learn from data.

15.5 Testing and Refining the Model

Testing and refining the model forms a critical phase in the development process of AI models. It provides the necessary insights to gauge the model's real-world performance and make necessary adjustments to improve its accuracy and reliability.

15.5.1 Model Evaluation

Once the model has been trained, it is vital to evaluate its performance to determine its effectiveness. This is generally done using a distinct dataset, referred to as the test dataset, which the model has never encountered during the training process. This independent evaluation serves to gauge how well the model has learned to generalize from the training data to unseen data.

To assess the model's performance, various metrics are utilized. In case of classification tasks, accuracy, precision, recall, and F1-score are commonly used metrics, whereas for regression tasks, mean absolute error (MAE) and root mean square error (RMSE) are typically employed. The choice of metric is often dictated by the nature of the task at hand and the specific needs of the project.

15.5.2 Error Analysis

Error analysis is a critical step that entails a close examination of the instances where the model has faltered. By scrutinizing the patterns in the model's mistakes, it is often feasible to pinpoint potential improvements to the data, the model, or both. It may help reveal biases in the dataset, areas of poor performance due to insufficient training data, or limitations in the current model architecture.

15.5.3 Model Refinement

Based on the findings from the model evaluation and error analysis, it is time to fine-tune the model. This refinement process may involve adjusting hyperparameters such as the learning rate, batch size, the number of layers in the model, etc. In some cases, it might necessitate collecting more data, further cleaning or augmenting the data, or altering the model's architecture to better suit the problem at hand.

The model refinement is usually an iterative process, often involving multiple rounds of adjustments and evaluations before the model's performance reaches a satisfactory level. Remember, the ultimate goal is to build a model that not only performs well on the training data but also generalizes effectively to unseen data. Striking this balance is crucial to circumvent overfitting (where the model performs exceedingly well on training data but poorly on new data) or underfitting (where the model fails to capture the underlying patterns in the data).

If the model's performance reaches an acceptable standard, it can finally be deployed. It can then be used to generate desired outputs or make predictions on new, unseen data, thus serving its ultimate purpose.

15.6 Epilogue

Congratulations on completing this critical chapter. By now, you should have a good understanding of the core concepts and steps involved in building a Generative AI system. From choosing the right tools to collecting and preparing your data, training your model, and refining its outputs, you've gained insight into the process that goes into creating AI that can generate new content. With this knowledge at your disposal, you're well on your way to developing your own Generative AI systems – should you choose to do so.

Made in the USA
Las Vegas, NV
02 December 2023

81901767R00085